Soft Gold

A History of the Fur Trade in the Great Lakes Region and its Impact on Native American Culture

Ted Reese

HERITAGE BOOKS, INC.

Published 2001 by

HERITAGE BOOKS, INC.
1540E Pointer Ridge Place, Bowie, Maryland 20716
1-800-398-7709
www.heritagebooks.com

ISBN 0-7884-1702-9

A Complete Catalog Listing Hundreds of Titles
On History, Genealogy, and Americana
Available Free Upon Request

CONTENTS

List Of Maps

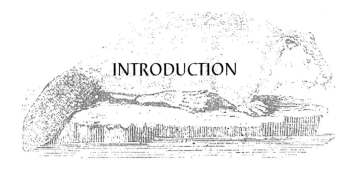

INTRODUCTION

With the discovery of the St. Lawrence River a gateway opened to the interior of North America, at whose heart lay the inland seas of the Great Lakes.

The first Europeans to enter this region came in search of the elusive Northwest Passage, the mythical trade route to the Orient. Rather than a westward leading sea, or the mineral wealth that was so abundant to the south, these men were to find riches in another form: beaver pelts, or "soft gold."

The pelt of the castor had been prized for centuries in Europe for the manufacture of hats. By the fifteenth century the European beaver had been hunted nearly into extinction. The St. Lawrence gave access to a land that was not only teeming with the animals whose fur was worth its weight in gold, but also with a ready-made labor force that was available to harvest these riches. For a small investment, any man could achieve riches in the short span of a year. This was the lure that first drew men to the wild lands of the St. Lawrence. Here the fur trade began that would dramatically affect the history of North America.

The fur trade, and the economic stimulation it provided, impacted both sides of the Atlantic with repercussions that have carried through to today. The cultural impact of this trade had its greatest effect on three peoples in North America: the British, the French and the Native Americans.

The consequences would be the most devastating for the Native Americans, resulting not only in a change in their social and economic life, but also in the total destruction of culture and the loss of their lands. For the French, the fur trade, or rather the struggle for its control, would end in a worldwide conflict and the loss of their empire in North America. For the British, the fur trade and the resulting struggle for its control would end in the acquisition of unimaginable amounts of land and, ultimately, the loss of its American colonies. For the colonists of North America, both British and French, the fur trade would lead to the establishment of two separate nations.

The Great Lakes country lay at the center of this struggle for control of the fur trade. The most direct access to the interior of the continent from the Eastern seaboard was by way of the St. Lawrence and the Great Lakes.

The effects of this struggle on the participants and their societies will be examined in the following pages, with particular attention to the Native Americans, who were the ultimate losers in the battle for cultural survival.

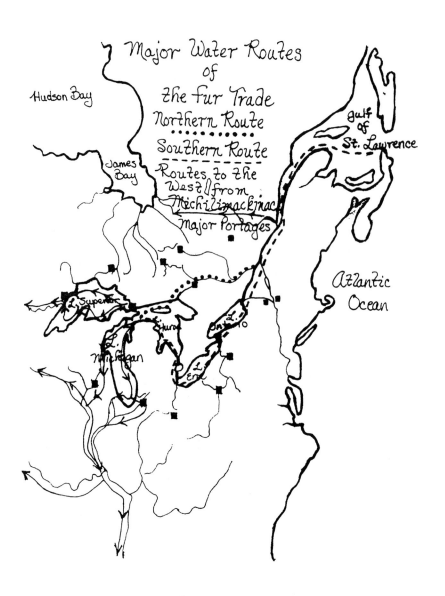

CHAPTER 1

The Great Lakes and The Fur Trade

We live in an age of modern travel: paved highways, railway service and air transport. To those of us who accept "next day delivery" as a fact of everyday life, the waterways, rivers and lakes are more of a barrier than a blessing. Our ancestors looked upon these same waterways as the highways by which to cross a continent. The river system of the St. Lawrence and the connecting waterways of the Great Lakes form a virtual highway by which people and goods can be transported to the interior of the mainland. From the Great Lakes, by short portage, the Mississippi, Missouri and Ohio River systems can be accessed, leading to the Great Plains and the far reaches of the interior.

The Native Americans knew of and used these river systems and their various tributaries long before the arrival of the Europeans. Native Americans conducted intertribal trade, and traveled to preferred hunting and fishing grounds through this vast network of waterways. Raiding war parties traversed these waters. The rivers and lakes, and the canoes that traveled on them, were as important to the eastern tribes as the horse would become to the western tribes after European contact.[1]

Substantial archeological evidence supports the theory of a pre-Columbian intertribal trade network. These established trade routes and connections later formed the basis for European contact routes. Such things as shells, food, and other

---

[1] Howard S. Russell, *Indian New England Before the Mayflower* (Hanover, N.H.: University of New England, 1980), p. 28.

commodities were transported by water from both coasts to the interior of the continent. (Ibid., p. 185.)

The uniqueness of the geography of the Old Northwest was highly important. This system of interlocking rivers and lakes made the fur trade not only possible but also profitable. The control of strategic points on these waterways was the key to the control and regulation of the trade. Because these water routes were of such vital importance to the commerce of the fur trade, those of major importance to the Upper Great Lakes will be examined.

The primary routes are those leading to and through the Upper Great Lakes. The St. Lawrence River is easily accessible from the Atlantic Ocean by passing between the southern tip of Newfoundland and the northern tip of Nova Scotia. The St. Lawrence is navigable for several hundred miles and leads directly into the interior of North America.

Once the traveler has negotiated the swift tidal currents and rapids of the St. Lawrence, he will find that the most easterly of Great Lakes, the broad open expanse of Lake Ontario, provides clear sailing for many days. The Falls of the Niagara forms the first barrier of any size to the traveler. The *voyageurs* carried their canoes and cargo over a backbreaking 20-mile portage before launching them again in the river above the falls. One enters Lake Erie from the Niagara River. By following the lakeshore northwest, the traveler will come to the mouth of the Detroit River and the Straits of Detroit. The route then swings north into Lake St. Clair and finally into Lake Huron. This is the most dangerous part of the passage. The western shore is indented by Saginaw and Thunder Bay, both of which are known for violent and unpredictable storms. The western shore was preferred over the eastern shore of the lake due to the shortness of the route.

The first of these great bays is that of the Saginaw. It would be foolhardy at best to cross the mouth of the bay in an open canoe. The safest route is to follow the southern shoreline of the bay to a point where the dangerous passage is broken up by two small islands, Charity and Little Charity. At this point the traveler is no more than ten miles from land at any point. If a storm were to strike, there would be hope of making a landfall. Once the bay crossing is completed, the traveler must swing to the northeast, rounding the far shore of the bay. The trip becomes easier from here until the shores of Thunder Bay are reached. This body of water, like the Saginaw Bay, is known for its violent and sudden storms. Having crossed Thunder Bay the course swings once again to the northwest towards the Straits of Mackinac.[2]

This is the dividing point of the lakes: to the north lies Lake Superior, by way of the St. Mary's River; to the west lies Lake Michigan and the rivers leading west to the Mississippi. The French explorers went west by this latter route—La Salle traveled by way of the Chicago to the Mississippi River, and Pere Marquette traveled through Green Bay to the Fox River and from there to the Mississippi. Access to the interior of the continent east of the Rocky Mountains can be gained by way of the Mississippi-Missouri system.

It would appear, from looking at a map, that the route through the Lower Lakes would be the most logical to follow. For various reasons this was not the case during much of the trading period. We must return once again to the St. Lawrence to follow the more highly trafficked route to the Upper Lakes.[3]

Approximately five miles west of the present city of Montreal, the Ottawa River joins the St. Lawrence, flowing from the west. There are no fewer than nine portages on the Ottawa, before the river turns north. The number of portages may be doubled by natural obstructions, especially after high water in the spring.

Leaving the Ottawa River where it is joined by the eastward-flowing Mattawa, upstream to the west, through a chain of small lakes to its headwaters, the traveler encounters

---

[2] *The Journal of Jonathan Carver and related Documents, 1766-1770*, ed. John Parker (St. Paul: Minnesota Historical Society Press, 1976), p. 70.

[3] Helen Hornbeck Tanner, *Atlas of Great Lakes Indian History* (Norman: University of Oklahoma Press, 1986), pp. 40-41.

five more major portages, the last of which covers several miles before reaching Lake Nipissing. From here travel becomes easier, as we follow the lake west to the French River then into Georgian Bay.

On Lake Huron the route follows the northern shore. The traders followed the channel between the mainland and Manitoulin and Drummond Islands.[4] Upon reaching the eastern end of the Upper Peninsula it is but a short passage across the Straits of Mackinac. If the traveler were to swing north, rather than south to the straits, he could portage the rapids of the St. Mary's River to Lake Superior and from there westward. The importance of this passage will be discussed in detail below.

The majority of the goods and supplies traveled to and from the interior by this northern route even after the southern route had been rendered safe for passage. The Ottawa route, though more arduous, was somewhat faster and freer from the prying eyes of government inspectors, who were always on the look out for contraband.[5]

Mackinac became the hub of the fur trade because of its central location in the Upper Lakes. With few exceptions all goods traveling either east or west passed through these straits. For this reason Mackinac, along with Detroit, played a vital role in the fur trade. Mackinac became the center of a vast web of trade routes stretching in all directions. It was from this point that the fur trade spread outward to the north and west. To the west, as we have already seen, lay the river systems of the Mississippi and a vast highway of rivers into the interior. To the north lay all of southern Canada to the Height of Land, which separated the Lake Superior watershed from that of Hudson Bay.

---

[4] Alexander Henry, *A Journal of Voyages and Travels in the Interior of North America* (Ann Arbor, MI: University Microfilms Inc., 1966), p. 35.

[5] General Thomas Gage to the Lords of Trade and Plantation 1763 (Manuscript Dept., W.L. Clements Library, Ann Arbor, MI.)

Once again, following the water route to the north and then west along the southern edge of Lake Superior, the traveler would come, by way of the Grand Portage near present-day Grand Portage, Minnesota, to the headwaters of the Pigeon River. Here the traveler enters an immense network of rivers and lakes. From the Pigeon River he would pass into Rainy Lake and the Lake of the Woods. Then he would make a portage to the Winnipeg River and on to Lake Winnipeg itself. Finally, by a series of portages to the north, he would arrive at Hudson Bay.

If the traveler were to portage west and then north from Lake Winnipeg, he would come to the Elk River and Lake Athabasca. From here, portaging once again, he would enter the Slave River and Great Slave Lake. A final series of portages would bring the traveler to the Mackenzie River and the Arctic Sea.[6]

A southern portage from Lake Winnipeg would have brought one to the Saskatchewan River from where, by crossing the Continental Divide, the traveler would reach the headwaters of the Columbia and the Pacific Ocean. This far-west country eventually became one of the prime trading grounds of the fur trade, either by direct contact or indirect contact with the Europeans by the Native hunters. The huge network of waterways that made up the Columbia River system became important to the British traders as a prime route westward when the trade expanded beyond the Great Lakes.

It must be remembered, however, that even as the actual trading of goods for furs moved westward, the all-important waterways of the Great Lakes remained of vital importance. Through the control of such areas as Niagara, Detroit, Mackinac, and for the British in the early trade, Oswego, the trade with the Native Americans was regulated to a degree.[7]

---

[6] Charles M. Gates, *Five Fur Traders of the Northwest* (St. Paul: Minnesota Historical Society, 1965), p. 102.

[7] O'Callaghan, *Documents Relating to the Colonial History of the State of New York*, Vol. VII (Albany: Weed, Parson, and Co., 1857), p. 637. (Hereafter cited

Archaeological evidence shows that intertribal trade flourished for centuries in North America and followed many of these same routes. Historical accounts bear this out through the records of early explorers who found European manufactured goods in the hands of Native Americans who had no outside contact.[8]

With such a trade system already in place, it was not difficult, after establishing a medium of exchange, to adapt the existing routes and forms of transportation to European uses. This, of course, was not immediately grasped by the Europeans.

The trade with the Native Americans was of secondary importance when first contact was made; of primary importance was a Northwest Passage. Exploration of the St. Lawrence began as a result of this search for a quick route to Asia. While the search, which continued into the nineteenth century, was to prove futile, it did lead to the establishment of the fur trade in North America.

The fur trade came about as a direct by-product of the exploration of North America. Early explorers, such as Hudson and Cabot, were searching for sources of ready wealth, such as gold and silver, as well as the Northwest Passage. In their contacts with the Native Americans they were given hope of the Northwest Passage with the stories of great seas to the west, but they were frustrated in their desire to find bullion.

They found instead of precious metals an abundance of wild life, in particular the beaver. Prized for centuries in Europe, where it had been hunted nearly to extinction, the beaver pelt became a means whereby the voyages of exploration could be financed. As a natural resource, beaver pelts were as great a source of wealth as either gold or silver. They required a minimum of investment by the trader. They were light and easy to transport. They required no effort on the part of the

---

as O'Callaghan, *DRCHSNY.*)

[8] George I. Quimby, *Indian Culture and European Trade Goods* (Madison: University of Wisconsin Press, 1966), p. 147.

trader to gather, as the work was already being done by a willing native population, and there was a ready market for the skins in the Old World. In the early years of the trade an inexpensive knife or a string of beads could be traded for several hundred dollars worth of pelts. The fur trade evolved from these early contacts with European technology. As the initial hope for a swift passage to the Orient faded, a reliance on the natural resources of this new land grew. The trade in furs went from a disorganized arrangement of accidental contact to an organized system of commerce. Sites such as the present-day city of Quebec became rendezvous locations where Native Americans and Europeans could conduct trade fairs.[9] At such fairs the Europeans displayed the products of their technology: items such as metal knives, hand-axes, cloth and jewelry. They exchanged these goods for the pelts of fur-bearing animals, in particular that of the beaver.

Large numbers of pelts could be garnered at first for any scrap of metal or worn cloth. The tastes of the Native Americans became more discerning as the trade progressed. Soon, both parties reached set values as the trade took on a more business-like nature. Over time, the sites of such trade fairs became occupied posts.

As the profits in the trade for furs increased, Europeans came to the New World for the sole purpose of conducting trade with the Native Americans. The establishment of these posts, particularly among the French in Canada, set the pattern for the trade—a pattern that would be followed until the trade ended.[10]

It was not long before the eastern coastline of North America was dotted with these small trading posts. While the

---

[9] W.J. Eccles, *The Canadian Frontier 1534-1760* (Albuquerque: University of New Mexico Press, 1964), p. 2.

[10] Frederick Jackson Turner, *The Character and Influence of the Indian Trade in Wisconsin: A Study of the Trading Post as an Institution* (Norman: University of Oklahoma Press, 1977), pp. 77-85.

harvest in furs did not reap the sudden riches of gold or silver, it did bring in sufficient revenue to warrant its expansion by the nations of Europe. The bulk of the trade was divided between furs, such as beaver and otter whose pelts were used in the production of hats, and deer hides, which were used in the manufacture of clothing, particularly those of tradesmen.[11] The trade in furs in the northern section of North America was divided between the French and the English by the middle of the seventeenth century. The English gained access to the St. Lawrence system through the colony of New York and its alliance with the powerful Iroquois League. The trade was of greater economic importance to New France than the English Colonies at this time, providing only twenty percent of the English export revenues.[12] It was this rivalry that sparked much of the friction between the two powers as both sought to dominate the "western trade," as it was then called.

From their very first contact with the Europeans, the Native Americas found their culture and existence changed for all time. The gathering of furs from the interior tribes became greater as the newcomers' demand for furs increased. Those Native Americans who found themselves in direct contact with the newcomers became the middlemen in the trade. The middlemen tribes would then send trading expeditions into the interior. These expeditions gathered furs from the more distant tribes. The trading parties exchanged goods for furs at highly inflated prices. Upon the return of these parties they once again traded the furs to the newcomers. For this reason most of the tribes were reluctant to allow the early explorers to travel very far inland.[13]

---

[11] O'Callaghan, *DRCHSNY*, Vol. VI, p. 1168.

[12] W.J. Eccles, "La Mer de l'Ouest: Outpost of Empire," *Rendezvous, Selected Papers of the Fourth North American Trade Conference, 1981* (St. Paul: Minnesota Historical Society Press, 1984), p. 6. (Hereafter cited as *Rendezvous.*)

[13] Eccles, *Canadian Frontier*, p. 105.

This system of middleman trade became one of the hallmarks of the Native American economy during the fur trade. This right was jealously guarded at all costs and became the reason for many intertribal conflicts, as well as inter-racial conflicts.

By the early eighteenth century the French had expanded the reach of their posts well into the Upper Great Lakes. The French gained control of the vital points in the Upper Lakes by a series of rapid moves. Such areas as Mackinac and Detroit were firmly under French control. The favored status of middleman had fallen to the Algonquin-speaking Ottawa, who would hold this position for the next one hundred years. Due to a tactical blunder by Champlain, the French found themselves cut off from the use of the southern passage to the Lakes.[14] Champlain made the mistake of allowing himself to be forced into taking the side of the Huron in a war with the powerful Iroquois League. The French firelocks turned the tide of battle, at least at first, in favor of the Huron. This was a political affront that the Iroquois would not soon forget.

Champlain had made a bargain with the devil, so to speak. By the mid-17th century the Huron nation had full control of all the furs coming from the West. Their hereditary enemies and near relations, the Iroquois, were the masters of the land to the south and to the southern gate to the Great Lakes. Champlain owed his economic allegiance and future to the Huron, and the Huron knew it. The French might have thought themselves superior to these naked savages, but they realized that in sheer weight of numbers the Hurons were the masters of the land north of the St. Lawrence. When the "request" for military aid came to the French commander, he had little choice but to acquiesce to the thinly veiled threat that underlay it. If the French were to have any future in this new world it would be at the suffrage of such savages.

The Iroquois, as a result of this armament shortfall, aligned themselves with the Dutch in Albany. The fur trade was

---

14 O'Callaghan, *DRCHSNY*, Vol. III, p. 507.

advanced through tribal alliances like this with the Europeans. The European colonies were able to vie with one another for the trade market by way of these relations with various middlemen and their allied tribes. This form of military alliance and economic dependency became another universal facet of the fur trade.

A series of intertribal wars broke out for control of the middleman trade because of these trade alliances between the Dutch/British-allied Iroquois and those tribes that had allied themselves with the French. The Iroquois, through either force of arms or political alliance, attempted to expand the territory under their control, to gain the greater share of this middleman trade. For a time, at the end of the seventeenth century, they were more or less successful, with the help of the British. These trade wars were to continue until the 1720's, ending with the last Fox wars, in which the last of the Iroquois' western allies were decimated by the French and the allied tribes of the Upper Great Lakes.

One of the major results of this series of intertribal conflicts and alliances was the formation of a British policy toward the Native Americans. In the case of the Iroquois this policy was referred to as the Covenant Chain, an idea first introduced by the Dutch and later adapted and expanded by the English. The Covenant Chain was a treaty of peace and brotherhood as well as a mutual defense pact and trade agreement, similar to the alliance that bound the five nations of the Iroquois together. It was through this association and a complex process of logic that the English government claimed the Northwest.[15] The Covenant Chain and its results will be discussed in greater detail later. It is sufficient at this time to point out that this policy was to be the basis for British-Native American relations during their occupation of the Northwest.

---

[15] Francis Jennings, *The Ambiguous Iroquois Empire* (New York: Norton and Co., 1984), pp. 8-9.

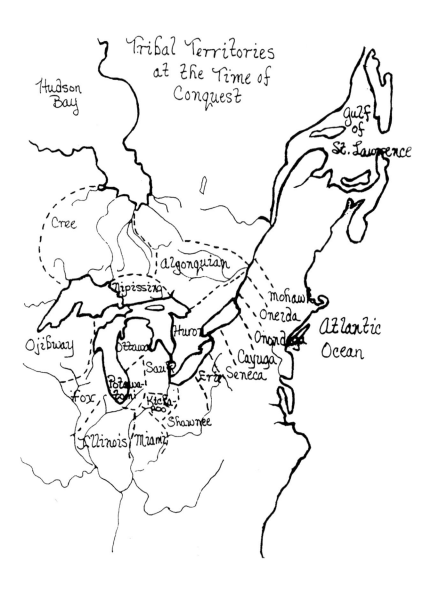

CHAPTER 2

The Native Americans

The love of liberty is innate in the savage; and seems the ruling passion of the state of nature. His desires and wants being few are easily gratified, and leave him much time to spare, which he would spend in idleness, if hunger did not force him to hunt. That exercise makes him strong, active and bold, raises his courage and fits him for war, in which he uses the same stratagems and cruelty as against the wild beast; making no scruple to employ treachery and perfidy to vanquish his enemy.

Jealous of his independency [sic] and of his property, he will not suffer the least encroachment on either; and upon the slightest suspicion, fired with resentment, he becomes an implacable enemy and files to arms vindicate his right, or revenge an injury.

—Henry Bouquet, 1763

It is fair to say that Bouquet's analysis is correct in as far as it goes. What Bouquet did not see, nor did many others at that time, was the complex economic and social relationships that existed among the Native Americans.

Long before the coming of the Europeans there existed a complex social and economic system of intertribal trade that spread over much of eastern North America. It was through this system of trade that European goods impacted native culture far from their source of origin. Tribes with direct contact with the Europeans would exchange goods for furs, and then they would exchange a portion of these same goods to tribes to the west for more furs.[16] Through this process European goods began to replace traditional commodities in intertribal trade. Where once the Huron of the eastern shore of Lake Huron had exchanged corn for dried fish with the Nipissing to the North, they now supplemented this trade with European goods for furs. They were able to increase their own purchasing power without increasing the time spent gathering greater quantities of fur themselves.

This is a greatly simplified example of a system that spread throughout eastern North America. This system of trade was to have great ramifications on the Native American way of life and culture. Before European contact the Native American had reached a state of equilibrium with his environment—that is to say, he was exploiting it to the best of his ability.

The Native American had a basic understanding of the ecology; he must live to some degree within the means of the land's ability to support him. This can be seen in the rituals and taboos that developed within the Native American culture governing his life and his relationship with the natural world.[17] The Native American was not a great conservationist in the modern sense of the word, but rather he understood the basic limits of his world. Mass exploitation of his environment was not necessary for his level of existence; in fact it was detrimental to his existence. As the Native American population grew and became sedentary, it was economically unsound to over-tax the environment by over-hunting to the point of extinction any possible food source such as beaver, moose, deer or bear—all of which were in high demand during the fur trade. It became necessary to shift the location of a village or family group according to the seasons, but these changes were done within well-defined areas. Each territory was under the specific control of a given group of individuals. (Ibid., p. 62.) These territories became more closely defined as

---

[16] O'Callaghan, *DRCHSNY*, Vol. IX, p. 633.

[17] Calvin Martin, *Keepers of the Game: Indian Animal Relationships and the Fur Trade* (Berkieley: University of California Press, 1978), p. 30.

agriculture began to take hold and land use became more intensified among the Native American people.[18] During this period when land usage among the native people was increasing, the first European contact was made. Now a new element was introduced into Native American life: the exchange of raw materials for advanced technological goods. This new source of materials allowed the Native American to exploit his environment as never before. Along with the means for this exploitation came the reasons. Animals that formerly had been hunted only as a source of raw material for personal use and for food had become a major medium of exchange.

This impact on the Native American's culture would forever change his world beyond his ability to control it. Once the Native American became a consumer of goods beyond his ability to manufacture, he became tied to a world he could not control. His culture was transformed from one of hunter-gatherer or hunter-farmer to that of hunter-trader-consumer. His former cultural ethics no longer fit his new way of life. The result was drastic change in the Native American world.

It is unfair to both the Native American and the Europeans to view the native people prior to contact as a peace-loving people living in harmony with each other. Inter-tribal warfare was the norm. This was practiced within the bounds of their cultural ethic and the limits of their technology. The native people were now given not only a reason, but also a way to be more efficient in war as well as the exploitation of the environment. These changes in long-standing cultural traditions were needed for their new position as consumers.

One of the practices that was carried over intact from the Native American pre-contact culture to the fur trade era, was the practice of gift giving. This was a very basic part of most Native American cultures. Ties of loyalty and kinship as well

---

[18] William Warren, *History of the Ojibway People Based upon Traditions and Oral Statements* (St. Paul: Minnesota Historical Society Press, 1981), p. 252.

as alliances were maintained through the giving of gifts.[19] The Native Americans maintained this system of material proof of friendship and alliance when interacting with the Europeans.

Native American culture had set guidelines that were followed in the giving of gifts. It was important that the person initiating the contact, or the person of greater social standing, give the larger gift. The Native Americans formalized their agreements and relationships through this giving of material goods.

This same giving of gifts would lead to great misunderstandings between the Native Americans and the Europeans. The custom became one of the major stumbling blocks between the British and the people of the Old Northwest during the British occupation of the territory.

It is unclear whether the French ever truly understood the cultural meaning behind the ceremonial giving of gifts; what the French were clearly aware of was their tenuous position in North America. Vastly outnumbered by their Native American hosts, the French were all too aware of the need for good relationships with the native people. The British, by comparison, viewed the native people as conquered enemies, and one does not give gifts to a conquered enemy.

For much of the seventeenth century the fur trade in the Great Lakes was in the hands of Native American middlemen. These middlemen were victimized by their European suppliers in the trade as the middleman's dependence on these suppliers grew. This was also true of the Native Americans who traded with the middlemen, as they became more dependent upon the goods the middlemen provided.[20] As the resources of fur-bearing animals were depleted in an area, the native people would turn to their neighbors for a new supply of furs, sometimes in trade but more often in war. (Ibid., p. 673.)

---

[19] Wilbur Jacobs, *Wilderness Politics and Indian Gifts: The Northern Colonial Frontier, 1748-1763* (Lincoln: University of Nebraska Press, 1950), p. 17.

[20] O'Callaghan, *DRCHSNY*, Vol. IX, p. 633.

Through this process of trade and warfare the position of middleman changed hands. As European contact spread west in the quest for more furs, so did the middleman position. A few tribes would be able to control the trade, either through military prowess or their abilities as traders or both. Foremost among these tribes were the Huron, the Iroquois and the Ottawa.

The Huron controlled the east-west flow of furs and goods for almost 100 years, because of their strategic location on the major western trade routes, and their firm alliance with the French. Huron control of the western trade was only broken after a series of devastating intertribal wars with the Iroquois, which resulted in the Huron being driven from their homeland.

The main control of the trade fell to the Iroquois. They had long since trapped out their own land, and relied on their position as middlemen for the Dutch, and later the English, to maintain their supply of European goods. They maintained their hold on the western trade for about 30 years before being forced into a secondary position by the French and their Algonkin allies. During this time period, the early part of the eighteenth century, the French made a concentrated effort to take physical control of the Great Lakes with the establishment of western posts.

The Ottawa now took over the dominant role of middleman in the trade. They held this position for the next 40 years.[21] The Ottawa were of the Algonkin-speaking people of the north and central Great Lakes. They had established themselves as traders long before the coming of the white man. A literal translation of their name, Ottawa, is "trader."[22] They were semi-nomadic hunter-gathers who took up basic agriculture about the time of contact. The Ottawa were expert canoe-men and fierce warriors. Both traits went far in expanding their

---

[21] O'Callaghan, *DRCHSNY*, Vol. IX, p. 673.

[22] W. Vernon Kinietz, *Indians of the Western Great Lakes*, Ann Arbor: University of Michigan Press, 1965, p. 235.

personal trade network to the south and west. It was with the help of the Ottawa and their neighbors, the Ojibway and Potawatomi, that the French were able to keep such a tight hold on the fur trade of the Great Lakes.[23] Through a system of trade alliances and trade prohibitions or boycotts, the Ottawa were able to control the flow of the majority of goods to the west.

A symbiotic relationship developed early on between the French and the Algonkin-speaking people. French records show that, contrary to popular belief, there was no great liking of one for the other. (Ibid., p. 623.) Both sides of this partnership viewed the other as a necessary evil. (Ibid., p. 372.) The French had need for the furs that the Ottawa were willing to obtain for trade, and the Ottawa had a ready market for the European trade goods beyond their own use. To the Ottawa, as well as the other tribes, control of such things as guns and ammunition meant a decided advantage in war, as well as an upper hand in peace negotiations. The tribe that controlled the trade could dictate terms to those who were dependent upon them for goods. The enmity of the controlling middlemen meant a lack of European goods to such western tribes as the Lakota.[24] This was an advantage that the tribes were not willing to relinquish to anyone, not even the Europeans. The struggle for control of this trade position would ultimately end in threatened or actual uprisings.

At the end of King George's War (1748) the tribes of the Great Lakes intimidated the French with such an insurrection. As the French made one last push to discover the elusive Northwest Passage, they extended their personal trade contacts beyond that of the Great Lakes tribes. Guns were being traded into the hands of the Lakota tribes, the hereditary enemies of the Algonkin. The result was near disaster for the French, who were menaced with uprisings at Michilimackinac and Detroit.[25]

---

[23] O'Callaghan, *DRCHSNY*, Vol. IX, p. 161.

[24] Eccles, *Canadian Frontier*, p. 125.

[25] O'Callaghan, *DRCHSNY*, Vol. IX, p. 644.

The threat of rebellion was not the only method that the people of the Great Lakes used to hold their trading partners in check. The Great Lakes tribes were able to keep the French and the British from achieving a firm hold on the trade by playing one side off against the other. (Ibid., p. 514.) After 1700, when the militant Iroquois were forced to sue for peace, the Ottawa were not above taking their business to the English at Fort Oswego.[26] They were able to maintain a balance of power in this way between the two European powers. The Algonkin would allow the French access to their country but when the price of goods was too great or the quality too poor, they could always go to the English, holding out hope for a change of alliance. The western tribes were able to hold the balance of power between the two European trade rivals.

The Native Americans, from this advantageous position, controlled not only the price of trade goods, but the quality and type of goods traded.[27] From 1700 until 1750 the true power of the trade lay in the hands of those tribes who controlled the middle trade. The Native Americans could maintain control of the trade as long as the Europeans were on the verge of, or at war. If one side or the other were to win the struggle for empire in the New World, as would eventually happen, then the control of the fur trade and their own destiny would slip from the Native Americans forever. It can be debated as to whether the Native Americans were truly aware of this fact or not. In the end it would appear to be a moot argument. What is apparent is the fact that at no time were the Native Americans intent on ending the conflict between the French and the English.

The tribes of the Great Lakes were firmly committed to the French in the ongoing wars of the colonial period. This was more economic reasons than for political. The Native Americans saw the Europeans as a necessary evil. The tribes knew that the English greatly outnumbered the French

---

[26] O'Callaghan, *DRCHSNY*, Vol. X, pp. 199-201.

[27] Eccles, *Canadian Frontier*, p. 125.

militarily, but the English were politically divided. The military records show that the native auxiliaries, while useful, were far from dependable for either side. They with few exceptions would fight, or at least remain neutral for a while, if offered enough gifts. The Ottawa, in a speech to Superintendent of Indian Affairs, Sir William Johnson, said in 1760 that they found it humorous that the both the French and the English were fighting to protect their (Ottawa) rights. The Native Americans realized that no matter what the outcome of the war between the European powers was, they would be the losers.[28]

---

[28] O'Callaghan, *DRCHSNY*, Vol. VII, p. 958.

CHAPTER 3

The French Involvement In The Fur Trade

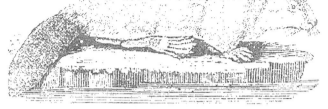

Paddles flashed in the sunlight as the great canoes raced for the shore. A ragged volley roared in salute from the beach. Wildly painted men charged into the surf to meet the onrushing fleet, as the paddlers leaped waist deep into the icy water to stop the speeding progress of their frail craft.

Such was the scene every spring at the far-flung fur trading posts of the Great Lakes. Every year the Native Americans brought their winter's catch of furs to such places as Detroit, Michilimackinac, St. Joseph, and La Baye to trade for the necessities of life. The traders left Montreal as soon as the ice had broken up on the St. Lawrence, and raced up river in a mad dash for the "soft gold" that was the mainstay of the economy of New France.

The fur trade in New France started along the St. Lawrence. Early traders brought their ships up river and established small temporary posts and reaped great profits in a very short time. This great influx of furs onto the market had such an effect that it had promised to ruin the trade if allowed to continue. In an attempt to control the trade and stabilize the fur market, the trade in furs became a royal monopoly whereby the king had the power to grant the sole right to trade to his favorites. While the monopoly system worked well in theory, in practice it was quite different. The king, by whose authority the system worked, was far from the forests of Canada, and his absolute rule meant little to the enterprising Frenchmen of Canada.

One major accomplishment during the French rule in Canada was the exploration of the vast interior. Under the

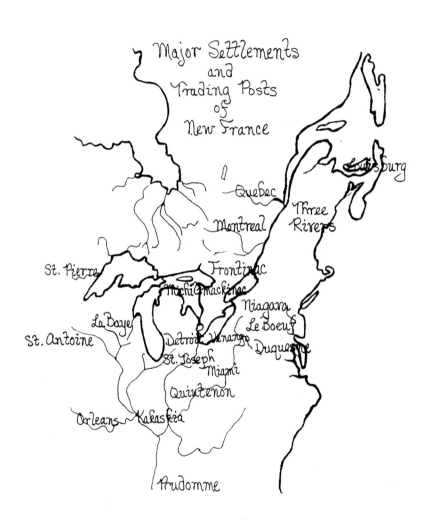

Major Settlements
and
Trading Posts
of
New France

Louisburg

Quebec

Three
Rivers

Montreal

St. Pierre

Frontinac

Michilimackinac

Niagara

La Baye

Le Boeuf

St. Antoine

Detroit Venango

Duquesne

St. Joseph

Miami

Quintenon

Orleans Kakaskia

Prudomme

monopoly system men such as Champlain, representing the One Hundred Associates formed by Cardinal Richelieu, expanded the boundaries of New France to the eastern shores of Lake Huron.

The profits of the newfound riches of the trade were not only destined for the coffers of the monopoly holders but for those of the king as well. M. Colbert, in a letter to M. Talon, the Intendent of New France in 1665, states that one-quarter of all the beaver taken by the West Indies Company and one-tenth of all moose hides were to go to the king. The West Indies Company had been given the monopoly on the fur trade, "by means whereof it paid the expenses of the country as it pleased."[29] France hoped in this way to make the colony profitable, as well as pay its own expenses, while the search for the elusive Northwest Passage continued.

The search for the Northwest Passage gave many an adventurer a way to bypass the Company's monopoly on the trade. Men such as La Salle received permission from the governor to explore and claim new lands in the name of the king, and were financed by private funds. La Salle and others saw this as an opportunity to enrich themselves through trade while carrying on their exploration.

The West Indies Company, like its predecessors, found it impossible to stop the illegal trade. Along with those adventurers who found semi-legal methods to enter the trade, there arose a new class of men in New France: the *coureurs de bois,* or "runners of the woods." This group, more than any other, extended the boundaries of New France, but they also almost proved to be the ruin of the colony.

A system of licenses was adopted as the monopoly came to an end. Under this system the king would issue twenty-five licenses each year with no one to have a license for more than one year. (Ibid., p. 159.) This was an attempt to give all those who could afford the license an equal share of the profits from the trade. In this way it was believed that the tide of illegal

---

[29] O'Callaghan, *DRCHSNY*, Vol. IX, p. 40.

traders could be stemmed. The license holder would be allowed to send twenty-five canoes, each with three men, into the Great Lakes. (Ibid., p. 160.) By royal edict all members of the government, clergy, and military were forbidden to take part in the trade in any way. (Ibid, p. 126.)

In addition to the licenses, trade fairs were to be carried on at Montreal and Quebec where the Native Americans could bring their furs. In this way the people of New France would be allowed to carry on a limited trade in furs at home. It was hoped that these trade fairs would also help to curb the illegal trade activities. But even the system of trade fairs was open to abuses. These abuses in the trade permeated all levels of government and society. When the Native Americans came to Quebec to trade, the governor would provide them with a guard for their protection. For this "service" they were charged a "fee" in beaver pelts that was set by the governor. In addition, the guards, who by royal edict were forbidden to take part in the trade, would take the Native Americans to their barracks where they would trade illegally for pelts. (Ibid., pp. 134-135.) With such far-ranging abuses of the system, control became impossible.

Some of the attitudes of the people of New France were due in part to the conditions of the land, much of which was poor for farming. Most people also had no intention of staying in the New World. It was for these reasons that the colony and the people of New France placed their economic hopes on the fur trade. Between 1675 and 1685, the amount of beaver fur alone taken in trade totaled 895,581 pounds. (Ibid., p. 287.) The lure of sudden riches caused many of the men of New France to defy the law and enter the Great Lakes trade.

The *coureurs de bois* were those who entered the fur trade without the necessary licenses. They came from all levels of society and were informally backed by almost everyone in the colony. Merchants who could not afford a license or whose license had expired financed such men with goods for a share of the profits. Only an estimate can be made as to the exact number of Frenchmen who entered into this illegal trade. The census of 1679 placed the population of New France at 9,400. (Ibid., p. 136.) Assuming that one-third of this population was male between the ages of sixteen and seventy, and that one-third of that number were involved in illegal trade, that would mean that roughly between 1,000 and 1,500 *coureurs* were leaving New France for the wilderness every year. While this is only a rough estimate, it gives as idea of the draw of this illegal form of commerce. The Native Americans also gave an indication of the number of Europeans involved. In 1679, the Native Americans complained in council with the governor, that they were being overrun by French traders. (Ibid., p. 131.) It is easy to see why so many of the young men of New France were drawn into the trade when we look at a report on their activities by Intendent Du Chesneau, who complained most bitterly about their activities. "A Coureur called La Taupine," he wrote, "traded 150 beaver robes in two days in a single village of the Ottawa." (Ibid., p. 132.) Each robe was made up of about ten hides. This would mean a gathering of about 1,000 hides in two days. In two days' work this man would see more of a profit than he could hope to make in a year of farming.

With this kind of incentive it is little wonder that so many men were willing to take the risk of death or prison to enter the trade. The problem was not helped by corrupt government officials, who were not only willing to turn a "blind eye" to much of the activities, but also were willing to share in the profits. In the same letter, Intendent Du Chesneau complained of having arrested a man he knew to be a *coureur*. Du Chesneau was shown a pass signed by the governor granting the coureur permission to enter the Great Lakes on a secret business with the Ottawa. (Ibid., p. 142.) Others were given hunting licenses, which they used as an excuse to travel up river. In that same year, 1679, the governor received 15,000 livres from a merchant of Rochelle for beaver furs. (Ibid., p. 135.) In his own defense the governor reminded the king that private trade was only illegal with the Ottawa. (Ibid., p. 154.) There was also, the governor complained, no way to stop the private trade: "Their numbers *(coureurs de bois)* increase every year, and the country is so open, and difficulty so great to ascertain precisely when they depart or when they return...."[30]

This inability to control the fur trade became a major problem for the French government, as it would later prove to be for the English. Since the abandonment of the monopoly system in the trade, the people of New France were expected to support themselves. With the great numbers of men slipping away to the wilderness, the colony began to flounder. Du Chesneau once again complained to the king of the conditions in New France:

> *The young men take to the woods in search of easy money. They are said to abandon their families and become acustom [sic] to the life of a vagabond and loafer, what little money they made on the trade, as much of it went to the merchants, was wasted on drink and fine clothes. The money that was to go to the support of the country was never paid.* [31]

As a result of this activity, all trading licenses were suspended. This, however, proved to be too little too late. Brigades of coureurs formed openly by the 1680's. The government attempted to put a stop to the actions of the coureurs, but they threatened to revolt. (Ibid., p. 131.) In an effort to stem the possible revolt an open pardon was offered to bring the coureurs out of the woods. This action met with only limited success. Once again, licensing for the trade had to be reinstated. This time the number of licenses issued (twenty-five) remained the same. (Ibid., p. 954.)

The problem of smuggling compounded matters for the French government. Many of the coureurs, as well as the licensed traders, found a better market for their furs in Albany rather than Montreal. The English were willing to pay higher prices for furs and the quality of their goods was superior to that of the French.[32] This manufacturing inequality was a factor in helping the English interests in the Great Lakes trade. The

---

[30] Eccles, *Canadian Frontier*, p. 203.

[31] O'Callaghan, *DRCHSNY*, Vol. IX, p. 133.

[32] *Wisconsin Historical Collections*, Vol. V, p. 117.

quality of English cloth was so superior to that of the French that the Native Americans would accept no other in trade. (Ibid., p. 118.)

As a result of this activity the colony of New York found itself in a unique position during this period. Due to the missionary efforts of the Jesuits, the Mohawk Nation had become divided roughly in half. Those who had converted to Catholicism lived at the north end of Lake Champlain near the St. Lawrence. The remainder stayed in their own country near their traditional allies, the British. Both groups were reluctant to declare war on their fellow tribesmen. The result was an uneasy peace between them that was to last until the outbreak of the Seven Years' War. This, along with the demand for English cloth by the Native Americans who traded with the French, allowed Albany to remain neutral during most of the colonial wars that rocked the English colonies during the seventeenth and eighteenth centuries. Albany became the major English fur trade center, as it had been for the Dutch before them.

The coureur de bois was not the only class to arise as a result of the fur trade in New France. Because of the unique form of transportation involved in moving goods and furs over long distances, a distinct group of men came into being: the *voyageurs*, or paddlers. The voyageurs were to become the backbone of the fur trade throughout its existence. The voyageurs were the "work horses" of the fur trade. They paddled the canoes hundreds of miles each year, transporting goods up the rivers and lakes and over long portages to the far-flung posts. Voyageurs were expected to keep up a speed of 60 strokes per minute, for 12 to 14 hours, stopping to rest only once every hour for 10 minutes. They would then return to Montreal or Quebec with the previous winter's catch of furs. For the most part they came from the lower classes of society. Many were illiterate farmers who took up work in the trade as it began to expand in the seventeenth century. Most individual voyageurs worked under a signed or "marked" contract, which stated his wages, the amount of weight he was to carry at each portage, his position in the canoe, and how far he was expected to travel. If a voyageur was to be allowed to trade, as many of them were, then the amount of goods he was to be allowed was also stated in the contract.[33]

As with everything else, there were regulations governing the use of these men in the trade. Every license holder had to list the names and place of residence for each paddler in his employ. Each man was to have a musket in his possession, for his own protection, and no more than four gallons of brandy were to be allowed per man. In addition, no crew list could be changed once it had been made up, nor could false names be entered on the rolls. This was often done to increase the allotted amount of brandy. The hope of the government was keep track of the individuals employed in the trade, as well as to regulate the flow of goods and furs in and out of New France. These same practices were to be adopted by the English.

The government of France was finally forced to give ground after a hundred years of attempting to regulate the trade. They had found that despite all laws, penalties, and royal decrees, it was impossible to control the flow of illegal traders to and from the frontier. By the middle of the eighteenth century there was little recourse but to make what profit they could from this illegal traffic; in an effort to do so, the command of military posts was sold to the highest bidder. In return for the command the government gave the officer all rights to conduct trade at his post. In addition, the government was to receive a percentage of all furs coming through the post. Officers would often form companies with members of their families as well as with the men under their command in order to raise the monies necessary to purchase a command. (Ibid., pp. 146-147.) In 1754, the commander of Fort La Baye at Green Bay requested thirteen canoe loads of trade goods be sent to him. The French force at this post consisted of one officer, one sergeant and four privates. The cost of the goods, billed to the officer, was 7,000

---

[33] Nute, *The Voyageur*, p. 8.

livres. The officer's share of the profits from this post was 15,000 francs. (Ibid., p. 145.)

This was the system of trade that the English were to inherit at the end of the Seven Years' War in America—a system so laced with corruption and spread over such an immense territory that it was impossible to regulate. Added to these difficulties were the inherent differences that evolved with the English fur trade.

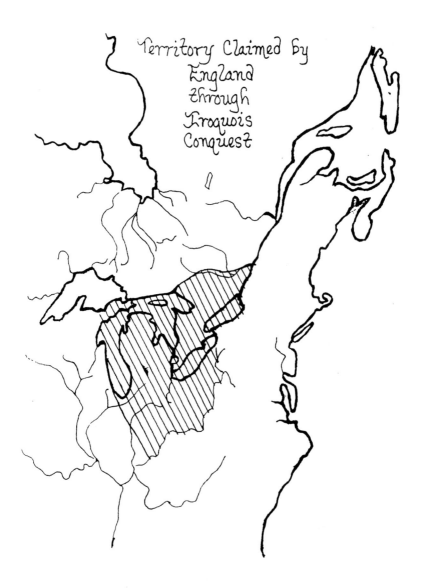

CHAPTER 4

The English Involvement In The Fur Trade

When you [English] first came to this land, you were like an old man, weak and feeble. You came to us and said 'let me warm myself by your fire brother, I will not take much room...'[34]

This is how the Native Americans metaphorically viewed the English. In many ways this was an accurate picture. The English entered the colonization of the New World late in comparison to the other European powers. In comparison to the French, and even the Dutch, the English could be seen as "weak old men," with their tiny colonies along the New England and Virginia coastline.

Not until they took possession of New York did the English make their presence felt in the interior of North America. When the Dutch ceded the colony of New Amsterdam and the Hudson River valley, the English gained a highway to the interior. Along with the colony, the English also inherited the "Covenant Chain" that the Dutch had formed with the powerful Iroquois League of nations to the west. The Covenant Chain was a metaphoric term for the trade agreement and mutual defense pact that the Dutch had with the Iroquois. This agreement provided the Iroquois with the guns and ammunition with which to conduct their trade wars with the Huron and the French. In return the Dutch were to receive exclusive trade rights to all Iroquois furs, and defense by

Iroquois mercenaries against the French and their allies. When the English took control of the colony, they were to base their future dealings with all Native American people in the eighteenth century on this Chain of Covenant with the Iroquois.

Using the Covenant Chain and their association with the Iroquois Nation, the English claimed the Old Northwest and the Great Lakes.[35] The Hudson and Mohawk Rivers formed a route of direct access to the lower Great Lakes. After establishing themselves in New York, the English started to seek their share of the wealth of furs that were flowing to New France. Through direct contact, as well as through their Iroquois middlemen, the English began to make inroads to the Great Lakes. By 1685 Governor Thomas Dongan of New York had sent a trading expedition to Michilimackinac for the purpose of opening trade with the western tribes. Much to the horror of the French, these interlopers were well received, due to the higher quality and lower prices of their goods.

However, this was not the first contact many of these western tribes had with English manufactured goods. They already had made direct or indirect contact with Hudson's Bay, as well as trade through the Iroquois acting as middlemen for the English. Some had even made the long journey to Fort Orange (present-day Albany) to trade with the English.

It was the Iroquois, however, who were of primary importance to the English and would remain so throughout the colonial period. Through the Iroquois and the Covenant Chain, the English carried on all their contacts with other Native American nations. The Iroquois played the role of conquering sovereigns of the native people, whether true of not. The English claimed that all the lands west of the island of Montreal to the eastern shore of Lake Michigan, south to the Ohio River and east to the Appalachian Mountains had been conquered by the Iroquois. In this way all the native people who occupied this land did so only by rights given to them by

---

[35] Jennings, *Iroquois Empire*, pp. 182-183.

the Iroquois. The Iroquois, being the vassals of the English through the Chain of Covenant gave the English direct claim to the whole of this territory. This idea formed the claim by the English to the Old Northwest, and would be the basis for their policies for the next 100 years. This also took all rights to these western lands and their resources away from the colonies, who claimed part, if not all of them by royal charter, and now gave control directly to the Crown.

The truth to the Iroquois claim to empire has long been debated. Whether it is true or not is unimportant for the purpose of this book. It is sufficient that the English believed it and upheld it, even in the face of direct denial by the western nations.

The other major agent affecting English policy was the Hudson's Bay Company, especially in the area of the fur trade. The Hudson's Bay Company established a monopoly that grew into a fur trade empire in the north. Its method of operation was to establish posts at key points and allow its customers to come to them. Whether by direct contact or through their middlemen, known as the "the Home Guard Indians,"[36] (those tribes who had taken up permanent residence near the company factories, as the bay posts were called), the Bay Company was able to tap the resources of the Upper Great Lakes as well as far into the Great Plains. Through this policy of limited contact the Bay Company controlled the flow of furs through its posts with a minimal amount of effort and little, if any, loss in profits. This system was well suited to the frozen north with its limited access, but as has been shown by the French attempts at monopoly, was unworkable in the Great Lakes. The English based their dealings with the Native Americans after 1763 on this "limited contact" point of view. Their total lack of understanding of the Native American peoples and their diverse cultures led to future problems.

---

[36] Arthur J. Ray, *Indians in the Fur Trade: Their Role as Hunters, Trappers and Middlemen in the Lands Southwest of Hudson Bay* (Toronto, Canada: University of Toronto Press, 1974), pp. 35-36.

This lack of understanding comes to the forefront when the rhetoric and the social patterns of the Native Americans are examined in more than a superficial way. While it is well understood that the Native American society was totally foreign to the Europeans, it was not widely understood that this social pattern was carried over in many forms to their dealings with outsiders—that is to say those outside their family or tribal group.

The family-kinship arrangement of the Great Lakes Algonkin was such that the parents were not seen as authority figures as they were in the European family, but rather as protectors and providers. These individuals did not have a ruling position over the family, but rather were there to guide the children and provide protection and food. In return the children were to give the parents loyalty and provide for them in their old age. Children were also to be "pitied," or as we would say, "cared for." Those who had no one to care for them were to be given "charity," or adopted into a family or clan.[37]

These same terms had a totally different meaning to the English. They meant subservience and dependence, rather than interdependence or service between members of a community. This fundamental misunderstanding, based on a cultural difference in word meaning and usage, would become one of the underlying bases of English policy during their occupation of the Old Northwest. The Native Americans ask the English to "pity" them by giving them fair treatment; the English took this as a sign of submission, rather than a request for fair treatment as an equal. When the Native Americans ask for "charity," the English understood this to mean weakness, rather than a request to be treated as an adopted equal.

Linked to this misunderstanding was the treaty of 1683 in which the Iroquois declared themselves to be subjects of the

---

[37] Bruce M. White, "'Give us a Little Milk': The Social and Cultural Significance of Gift Giving in the Lake Superior Fur Trade." *Rendezvous*, p. 191.

king of England.[38] (Ibid., p. 250.) It was doubtful that the Iroquois had a full understanding, in the European sense, of what it meant to be the subjects of a foreign power or king. If they had, it is doubtful that they would have submitted to such an agreement, regardless of the consequences. Once having done so, however, the way was open for the English to establish a rightful claim of conquest over the western lands. In this way the English view of the western tribes was forever colored. The western nations would always be seen as a conquered people who were indirect subjects of the kings of England. (Ibid.) This concept guided English policy most heavily in the early days of their occupation of the Great Lakes. It was also a contributing factor to the Native American uprising of 1763, known as Pontiac's Rebellion.

The French had always seen themselves as guests in the Great Lakes. Despite what they might say to the English, the French were painfully aware that they held their posts in the west by keeping the good will of the Native Americans. To treat their "hosts" as a conquered people was to invite destruction. The French claim to land extended no farther than the firing range of a French musket beyond the walls of their posts.

These fundamental differences and cultural mis-understandings, along with the lack of regulation of—or, rather, the inability to regulate—the fur trade, formed the basis of the English occupation of the Great Lakes region. These very differences changed the people involved in the fur trade until, ultimately, the native culture crumbled.

---

[38] Jennings, *Iroquois Empire*, p. 250.

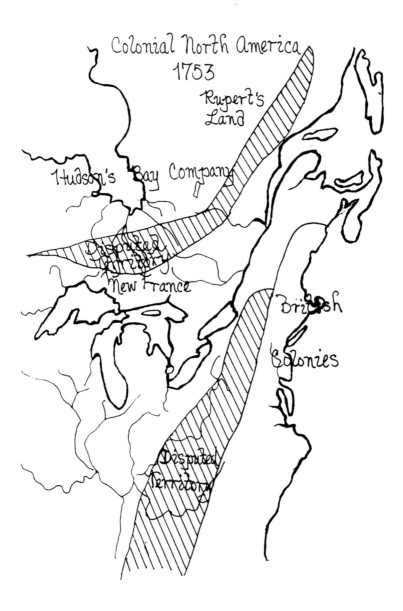

CHAPTER 5

The Seven Years' War in America And The Indian Uprising

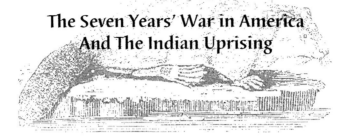

By 1754, the French had completed a chain of forts from Niagara to the Gulf of Mexico, while the English were hemmed in along the East Coast. The fur trade from the west had been cut off with the destruction of Pickawillany in present-day Ohio and the death of their strongest ally, the Miami chief "Old Britain."[35] The French now occupied the forks of the Ohio, there by controlling the major water route west. The smuggling that had always gone on from Montreal to Albany was now stopped.[36] The French were determined to push the English out of the western trade once and for all. The conditions were right for the final decisive war for the control of the fur trade in North America.

In the years leading up to the Seven Years' War, also known as the French and Indian War, both sides had showered the Native Americans with gifts in attempts to sway their allegiance. These attempts were met with mixed results at best by both the French and the English. Both sides were well aware of the benefits of native auxiliaries. While they might be "sunshine warriors" at best, their knowledge of the country and the fear they were capable of instilling in European troops far outweighed their desertions.

Both sides paid dearly for these Native American troops, most often in cash. The Stockbridge Indians, famous for serving with the American partisan, Robert Rogers, were paid

---

[35] Peckham, *Pontiac*, pp. 101-02.
[36] O'Callaghan, *DRCHSNY*, Vol. V, p. 552.

four shillings a day. This was a fortune when compared to the six pence a day paid the British line troops. Along with wages for their services, the Native Americans were paid bounties for scalps and prisoners. These bounties ranged from twenty pounds to fifty pounds for a scalp, depending on the commander, and fifty pounds to one hundred pounds for a prisoner. As the war escalated so did the cost of keeping the Native American allies.

The war had severe economic effects on all sides. The main theater of operation became the Lake Champlain corridor. This was the route that had been used by smugglers to bring furs and trade goods back and forth between Montreal and Albany. The loss of this trade had a dramatic effect on the economy of the colony; Britain was now being deprived of one-third of its profits from the fur trade. The war hurt the French trade even more. As their need for manpower to fight the war grew, the French offered pardons to the *coureurs de bois*. As more and more traders left the field to fight, the trade in furs slowed to a trickle.

The Native Americans were affected as well, but not by the loss of trade goods. The gifts and plunder of war had begun to take the place of trade goods. The war depleted manpower from the tribes. Increasingly, those left behind had to depend on the Europeans for food, as there were fewer men to hunt for their families.

Disease was another devastating effect of the war on the Great Lakes tribes. Victorious warriors who had plundered the graves of the English at Fort William Henry for scalps brought back smallpox, which swept through the tribes like wildfire. It would be generations before the Great Lakes tribes would recover from the effects of that plague.[37]

As the war raged on and the flow of furs from the New World slowed, the prices on the European markets went up. The law of supply and demand had taken over. Fur prices had reached an all-time high in England and France. The war had

---

[37] *Bougainville's Journals*, p.116.

become one of economics as well as military actions. The tight restrictions that had typified the French fur trade until the early 1700's had been dropped completely in an effort to increase the supply of furs.[38] These liberal measures had little effect however, as most of the native hunters had abandoned trapping in favor of the gifts and glory of the battlefield.[39]

The English fur trade economy was in even worse shape. Cut off as they were from any western trade and from their own middlemen, the Iroquois, who now made up the bulk of their native allies, the English trade in furs had stopped by 1759. Currency began to play a larger role in gift giving. The Native American was becoming more conscious of the workings of the Europeans' world. The effect of this was an increasing drain on the treasuries of the colonies as well as those of France and England.[40]

After six long bitter years the war in North America nominally came to a close with the fall of Quebec. Although it was another year before Montreal itself would fall, word was sent west that the French had lost. This was the worst of all possible results for the tribes of the Great Lakes. It had been in their best interest to have a state of hostility exist between the two European powers. With the loss of the war by France, the balance of power had now shifted into the hands of the English. It is pure conjecture to speculate if the tribes of the Great Lakes would have fared any better under French domination than English. Both powers saw the Native American as a necessary evil at best.

With the shifting of power in the fur trade from the hands of the Native Americans to the English, the fur trade went from a seller's to a buyer's market. The results of this shift in market emphasis had a devastating effect on the native economy of the Great Lakes. Although the French had not been driven totally out of North America, they were now relegated to a secondary

---

[38] Eccles, *Canadian Frontier*, pp. 179-81.
[39] Thwaites, *Early Western Travels*, p. 16.
[40] Jacobs, *Politics*, p. 38.

position. Deprived of direct access to the Great Lakes and the Ohio River valley, the French fur trade in the north fell into ruin. Although they tried for the rest of the century to reestablish themselves as a major trading power in this country, their attempts were poor at best.

With the defeat of the French, it was back to business for the English. But it was not to be business as usual. There were vast new territories to govern, newly conquered peoples to bring under the British rule, and a huge amount of resources to exploit. The way was finally open to the west. The riches of the Great Lakes and the land beyond were not theirs for the taking—or were they? The French were going to cede these lands to the English without the consent of their former allies. This meant very little to the English who saw themselves as conquerors-by-proxy by way of their sovereignty over the Iroquois. As the English were to find out, this was a sovereignty that may have worked in theory but not in practice.

The first Englishmen to enter the Great Lakes region after the French and Indian war were fur traders such as Alexander Henry and Ezekial Solomon, who were eager to make their fortunes regardless of the risks. They were quick to find that while the French were willing to admit defeat, their former allies were not. The Chippewa told Alexander Henry at Michilimackinac that while the French may have been defeated and given up their lands, the Chippewa, Ottawa, and others had not. They saw these traders as enemies to be killed and plundered. To the Native Americans, only blood or gifts with which to appease their dead would put and end to the fighting. The timely arrival of English troops at Michilimackinac was mostly responsible for saving the traders' lives. This was not peace, only a cease-fire.

The problems the English had with the Native Americans were not confined to the new territory they had gained by war. Their former allies, the Iroquois, were beginning to grumble about their treatment at the hands of their friends. For years the traditional lands of the Iroquois had been eroded away by illegal and unscrupulous land deals. The English dependence on the Iroquois as middlemen ended with the war.[41] (Ibid., p. 128.) The once great Iroquois confederation began to break up with the friction of the war. Many of the Mohawks, formerly England's staunchest ally, had been proselytized by French missionaries and had moved to Canada.[42] Many of the Western Seneca had broken off from the alliance to form a tribe to the south known as the Mingos.[43] With the breakdown of the once-mighty Iroquois League came the breakdown of the Covenant Chain.

In July 1760, a small group of Iroquois led by Seneca chiefs appeared at a Wyandot village near Detroit. A council was called between the Seneca and their hereditary enemies the Wyandot, Chippewa, Ottawa, and Potawatomi. The Seneca proposed that all past hostilities be forgotten and that they unite against their common enemy the English. The Seneca offered to attack Fort Pitt and Fort Niagara, if their would-be allies would attack Fort Detroit. While the Wyandot may have been willing to listen to such a proposal, it is unlikely that they were willing to forget that it was the Iroquois who had driven these former Hurons from their home. In response to the Iroquois alliance request, the Wyandot went to Captain Campbell, the British Commander at Detroit and revealed the proposed conspiracy.[44] This action averted near disaster at this time. But the unrest that had been seething between the Native Americans and the Europeans for years was about to explode.

Cultural misunderstandings and shortsightedness of the British high command caused this explosion. Sir Jeffrey Amherst had proven himself to be a brilliant commander during the war. He was able to snatch victory from the jaws of defeat and overcome seemingly insurmountable odds. General Amherst saw the Native Americans as a necessary evil—they

---

[41] Henry, *Voyages*, p. 128.

[42] O'Callaghan, *DRCHSNY*, Vol. IX, p. 577.

[43] O'Callaghan, *DRCHSNY*, Vol. VII, p. 126.

[44] James Sterling's Letter Book, 1761-1777, W.L. Clements Library, Ann Arbor, MI, p. 24.

were useful in war and essential for conducting the fur trade. When the war ended Amherst saw the giving of gifts as paying the Native Americans for doing nothing. Amherst thought it best that gift-giving be kept to a minimum. In this way he planned on encouraging the Native Americans to become productive, by filling their needs through trade rather than by handouts from the king. General Amherst had a great dislike for giving gunpowder to the natives. He saw this as providing them with a way to cause trouble.[45]

What the General did not understand, and refused to accept, was that without the supplies of powder and shot that the natives had grown used to under the French, they could not hunt for their families and for the fur trade too. They did not see themselves as a conquered people, and expected that the English would "pay" for the use of their land just as the French had done. It was this mistaken belief on the part of the Native Americans, coupled with the economic bankruptcy of the Great Lakes tribes at the end of the Seven Years' War, that would bring rebellion.

Who was responsible for the revolt? Whether it was led by one man, Pontiac, or whether it was a popular uprising, is not important in this book. What is important is that it happened, and it had repercussions on the fur trade.

By the spring of 1763 the economic pressures that had started to build with the fall of New France had come to the point of explosion. The tribes of the Great Lakes and those as far east as the Appalachians rose up in force against the English occupation. By the end of that summer the British foothold in the west had almost been wiped out—Forts Detroit, Niagara, and Pitt managed to hold out. In the end it was the Native Americans' own lack of organization and inability to carry on a long siege that defeated them.

The greatest effect of this crushing defeat on the Native American tribes was to end their resistance to the English for all time. If they had not been conquered with the fall of New

---

[45] Amherst Papers, 7:97.

France, they were conquered with the signing of the Treaty of Paris. The English had subdued the Native tribes by force of arms. And it was thought by many in the British military that they should be punished in the most severe manner for their revolt.[46] Fortunately for all involved, this course of action was never followed; terms were arranged making the British the true sovereigns of the Great Lakes.

---

[46] Amherst Papers, 7:90.

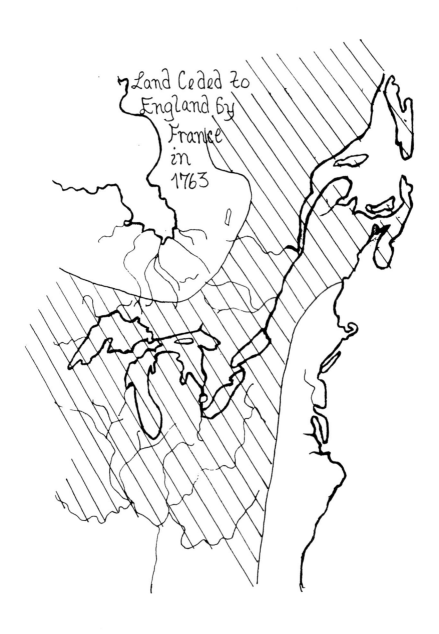

Land Ceded to
England by
France
in
1763

CHAPTER 6

The British in the Northwest

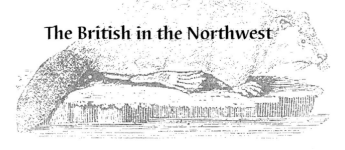

If you remember right I told your Lordships, that the whole system of our Indian Affairs was on a wretched footing throughout all America...

—Edmond Atkin, 1755

This was the observation of Edmond Atkin, a merchant of the Indian trade from Charleston, in his report to the Lords Commissioners for Trade and Plantation in 1755. These commissioners made up the advisory board that oversaw the operation of the colonies for the king, and held final say in the regulation of all trade. Atkin contended that if the English did not show a more unified front in dealing with the Native Americans, their cause in America would be lost. His seventy-page report condemned the British as a whole for their treatment of the Native American people. Along with his report, Atkin submitted a plan that he believed could rectify any problems in dealing with the Native American people. In essence Atkin's plan was highly commendable. In practice it was unworkable.

It called for the traders to be men of "honest repute and sober life..." and that they deal fairly with the Native Americans.[47] He also wanted a fixed rate of exchange to be set for all trade to prevent any fraud. (Ibid.) While these ideals

---

[47] Wilber Jacobs, ed. *The Appalachian Indian Frontier: Edmond Atkin's Report and Plan of 1755* (Lincoln: University of Nebraska Press, 1967), p. 86.

were commendable, they were impossible to regulate, even in 1755. By 1760 they had become unthinkable. The one part of Atkin's plan that was put into effect was the suggestion for two Superintendents of Indian Affairs, one for the territory north of the Ohio and one for those lands to the south. It was to Sir William Johnson that the Superintendency of the northern district was to fall. Thus, the position given to him by General Braddock in 1755 became a permanent one.

Sir William Johnson was a logical choice for this position. No one in the northern colonies had done more to endear himself to the Native Americans than Sir William. His long-standing ties with the Iroquois nation, in particular with the Mohawks, had given the English their strongest military ally throughout the colonial wars. Johnson was also respected, if not liked, by the tribes of the Northwest. Though he admired the Native Americans, Johnson was also practical about their relationship with the English. Publicly he would say anything, within reason, that they wished to hear while privately he knew that in the end they must be subjugated to the rule of England.[48] It would be through Johnson and his handpicked deputies that the fur trade in the Great Lakes would be regulated.

This regulation was to prove an undertaking of monumental proportions. While in theory it was fine to say that there would be fixed rates for the trade, in practice such price regulation became impossible. A trader could be forced to put up a nominal bond as security and to take an oath that he would abide by the rules and regulations set down by the crown. (Ibid., p. 850.) But once beyond the limits of civilized authority it was up the trader himself to stay within those regulations. This was a problem that had plagued the French throughout their reign in North America and would continue to plague the English.

One of the major contributing factors to the problem of British regulation of the fur trade would be that of attitude. The

---

[48] O'Callaghan, *DRCHSNY*, Vol. VII, p. 869.

attitude of the English to the Native American was in many ways radically different from that of the French. In the eyes of the British high commanders who were responsible for the political governing of the new territory, the Native Americans were merely the gatherers of a natural resource. As such, they were seen as having no more rights than any other common laborer, if as many. This policy was followed by all those who were to govern the new territory during the English occupation.[49]

The policy of the Lords of Trade in London was quite different. Officially the Lords of Trade and the king viewed the Native Americans as a sovereign people, but at the same time they were seen to be royal subjects, but without the rights of Englishmen.[50] This paradox in how the crown saw a group of people was not unique to the Native Americans. At various times throughout the history of the British Isles, groups such as the Irish, Scots, and Welsh had this same status. It would appear that such standing was beneficial in dealing with such problems as land ownership and individual rights under the law.[51] For example, no one was allowed to purchase land directly from any individual or group of Native Americans except the king or his agents. Yet if the crown found it needful to acquire land claimed by Native Americans, it was not necessary to purchase it, but rather merely claim it by right of conquest. In another case, the Native American was subject to English law as a royal subject, but he had no redress of grievance before the court, as he was a member of a foreign nation.[52] In this way the British deprived the Native American of any rights save those that were of use to the crown.

The question of authority further complicated matters in dealing with Native Americans. By royal decree only the Superintendents of Indian Affairs, or their agents, were to deal

---

[49] James, *License*, p. 125.

[50] Nicholas P. Canny "The Ideology of English Colonization From Ireland to America," *William and Mary Quarterly*, 3rd. ser. XXX (1973), p. 84.

[51] O'Callaghan, *DRCHSNY*, Vol. VII, p. 853.

[52] O'Callaghan, *DRCHSNY*, Vol. VI, p. 968.

directly with the native peoples. But under the provisions of royal colonial charters any Royal Governor, or his appointed agent, could deal and treat with a sovereign prince of a non-Christian nation who was not at war with the crown.[53] This gave the Royal Governor of any colony the perfect right to make treaties independent of the crown, not only with the Native Americans of his own territory but those of any other territory. As a result agents of such colonies as New York and Pennsylvania were entering the Great Lakes in an attempt to establish trade relations with the tribes there.[54] By royal decree only the superintendent had the right to issue licenses to traders. But, once again, every royal governor had the right to license individuals to conduct commerce to the benefit of their colony.

Another area of conflict that went well beyond the role of both the superintendent and the royal governor was the right to give gifts to the Native Americans. The superintendent, as the king's representative, was allowed to give gifts, but by charter so were the governors. To further complicate things, the military was also authorized to give gifts. In the area of the Great Lakes, the funds for the giving of presents to the Native Americans were to be controlled by the military governor. This meant that the funds needed by the superintendent for giving gifts during councils and treaty negotiations were controlled by the military, whose interests were often different from those of the superintendent. (Ibid., p. 953.)

After 1763 the crown, in an effort to increase the revenue from its newly gained lands by allowing more traders, decreed that any English subject could obtain a license to trade in the Great Lakes, provided they could supply the needed security bond. This bond was to be held as an assurance of good conduct on the trader's part. In theory, this would seem to be a sound practice, but once again unworkable. With so much territory in which to disappear, and so few people to watch

---

[53] O'Callaghan, *DRCHSNY*, Vol. IV, p. 291.
[54] O'Callaghan, *DRCHSNY*, Vol. VII, p. 571.

over the traders' business practices, each trader was left to the dictates of his conscience.

The bond requirement was not only a hollow pledge, at best, but more often than not there was nothing to back it up. A prospective trader had only to present a paper certifying that he possessed property in the value of five hundred pounds to receive his license. The actual cost of the license was only two shillings. Rather than regulating the trade, this left it open to any man who could raise the licensing fee.

For any person who could not raise the fee or convince the officials that he owned real property worth five hundred pounds, there was always the option of acting as the agent of those who possessed a license, and there was no shortage of these individuals. Many merchants in England and the colonies, as well as Canada, were in the possession of trading licenses. This gave every unscrupulous individual, whether he had experience or not, a chance to enter the fur trade at no financial risk to himself. There were also a large number of foreigners—French, German, and Dutch—who wished to enter the trade and were in need of an English representative to purchase their license for them. Whether merchants or traders, these men were not interested in the scruples of the men who worked for them, as long as they made a profit. The Great Lakes country was flooded with would-be traders, all of whom were out to make their fortune.

With the inheritance of the vast territories that had been New France came another problem for the British government—that of the French citizens. Once again the government faced a dilemma. This one was easily handled by the Quebec Act of 1774. This act in fact gave the French inhabitants of Canada the right to carry on their lives as before.

During the eleven years before the Quebec Act was enacted, the French population was in limbo. They were a people without a nation or without rights, except those given to them by their conquerors.

The French, by right of prior occupation, had been long established in the Great Lakes fur trade. This long period of contact gave the French a decided advantage over their English competitors. This was a fact that was not lost on the English. It was an advantage that the French were more than willing to pursue if given the chance. Yet their new status in their own country, that of non-citizens, gave them few rights and fewer opportunities to press this advantage. In an effort to restrict any French activity it was suggested that the French who wished to enter the fur trade or continue working as traders, not be allowed to travel farther west then the mouth of the Ottawa River.[55] This was quickly seen as an unsound business practice. The French Canadians were necessary to the trade for their knowledge of the Native Americans. It was also suggested that no person of French descent be allowed to hold a position greater than that of clerk with any trading company. (Ibid.) In this way any possible traffic with the French in Louisiana could be stopped. This proved to have only limited success, as many of the French traders took on English partners whose names appeared on the license. (Ibid., p. 201.) For a time, at least, the French owners were able to retain nominal control over their trading businesses. The English were able to take control of the fur trade at its center, because of their greater capital and the control of the licenses. During the eleven years prior to the institution of the Quebec Act of 1774, the British had succeeded in taking complete economic and political control of the Northwest. The French had been placed into the role of second-class citizens during this time with only the limited rights of a conquered people. The attempts at restricting the French activity resulted in havoc on the frontier. Old hatreds died hard and the added restrictions made matters worse. Many of the English traders complained that the French traders were using their influence with the tribes to their advantage. The French claimed that the English would cheat the natives, and that they would steal their lands.[56] Some of the French went so far as to incite the Native People to attack the

---

[55] O'Callaghan, *DRCHSNY*, Vol. VIII, p. 422.
[56] O'Callaghan, *DRCHSNY*, Vol. VII, p. 960.

English traders as a way of discouraging others from trading in an area.[57] This action is often seen as the reason for the Native American uprising of 1763, or Pontiac's Rebellion. Whatever their methods, however, they were unsuccessful — the English kept coming. In the end it was not laws nor military power that were to force the French into a secondary position in the fur trade, but rather greater finances and sheer weight of numbers.

With the direct access that the St. Lawrence afforded the English merchants, the trade centers began to shift to the north and west. Albany, which had been the traditional center of English trading endeavors, was replaced by the traditional French centers at Montreal and Quebec. This added to the growing friction between the French inhabitants and the English. Along with being deprived of their rights as Frenchmen, and having restrictions placed on their involvement in the trade, the French merchants were deprived of their traditional markets in the mother county as well as many of their normal sources of goods.

English and Scots soon filled the void that was left by these French entrepreneurs. Such men as Alexander Henry, Alexander Mackenzie, Peter Pond and David Thompson became leaders of the English fur trade.

The shift in the trading centers was not restricted to the St. Lawrence area alone. Michilimackinac grew in importance as the focus of the trade in the interior began to move westward. It had been just one more of the far-flung posts in the French chain during the period of French occupation. Under the British occupation Michilimackinac became the gateway to the western trading grounds. This became the last point of possible inspection and regulation of trade goods. Michilimackinac reached its height as a trade center during the time of British occupation. All westward-bound canoe brigades were to stop there before going into the western lands. If the trader wished to avoid the prying eyes of the officials, however, he could still run the north passage around St. Joseph Island to the St. Mary's

---

[57] Eccles, *Canadian Frontier*, p. 125.

River. It was a risky trip, but if the trader timed his passage, usually under the cover of darkness, and was lucky he could slip through the rapids and past the small garrison at "the Sault" (the rapids). (Ibid., p. 187.)

Michilimackinac grew to even greater importance as the trade became more sophisticated with the introduction of large ships, such as John Askin's sloop the *Welcome*, for the transportation of goods and furs. Michilimackinac's strategic location allowed for the transfer of goods and furs to take place at a central location in a larger volume than ever before, without traveling to the fur centers of the St. Lawrence or New York. As a result, traders were able to venture farther into the interior, and trade for more furs. Michilimackinac's growing importance as a trade center affected the lives of the Native Americans living in the area. The Ottawa, who had always been semi-nomadic, were taking up permanent residence at the Straits of Mackinac. This move started before the Seven Years' War; by 1763 the resident tribe had nearly doubled in size, as they found it more profitable to raise corn to feed the traders and the fort's garrison. This was only the beginning of a major shift in the lives of the Native Americans of the Great Lakes as a result of the British occupation.

Pressure on the population of fur-bearing animals increased as new traders flooded into the lake country to claim their share of the riches. The newcomers were not content to wait for the meager harvest of the lakes or wait for the fickle whim of the middlemen. The English traders flooded into the lakes and beyond. This area had always been the province of the Native American middlemen, and was not a region that they were willing to give up without a fight. If they surrendered this territory to the English it would mean the loss of control of the vital western trade, and all the carefully established systems of trade alliances and boycotts. A breakdown of the middleman system would mean that anyone who had furs to trade would be on an equal footing with his enemies. The delicate balance of power that had been the bulwark of the Native American politics and economy would be destroyed forever.

For years the Ottawa and other tribes of the Great Lakes had been careful to make sure that certain tribes, such as the Lakota, did not have regular direct access to guns and ammunition. The Mandan and the Arickara had blocked the Lakota from direct trade with the French in St. Louis to the south,[58] just as the Ottawa and their allies had blocked trade to the east and north. The French, in 1745, had tried to bypass the middlemen of the Great Lakes with disastrous results that had almost led to the end of their occupation of the lake country. In 1773, however, the power of the lake tribes was broken, and the tribes were powerless to stop the flood of goods and traders headed west.

The native people had found that they lacked the manpower to stop the traders during the uprising ten years earlier. They could not hope to stop them now that the English were firmly entrenched and were the major suppliers of the goods upon which they were now so dependent. The tribes of the Great Lakes, like others before them, had lost their niche in the fur trade as major traders. As further social and cultural changes took effect, the Native began to fill other roles in the fur trade. They found work as guides, canoemen, interpreters and hunters for the westward-bound brigades of traders. These were the positions that had been held by the French Canadians, but as the trade outstripped the areas of their knowledge and contact, they were finding themselves replaced by their one-time trading partners. The French were now being forced out of the trade from the bottom as well as the top.[59]

The result of this shift in the labor market, along with the change in transportation represented by the use of large ships rather than canoes on the lakes, was to force the French Canadians to move westward or south to Louisiana and St. Louis. In either case they found themselves being forced further out into the fringes of the trade.

---

[58] O'Callaghan, *DRCHSNY*, Vol. V, p. 131.
[59] O'Callaghan, *DRCHSNY*, Vol. VII, p. 961.

If the economic outlook for the French traders was bleak, it had become a boom for the English traders. In the first years of the English occupation the trade in furs was at an all-time high; at the same time, so were robbery, murder and corruption. (Ibid., p. 965.) In an effort to gain a larger share of the profits, the traders would do anything. Sir William Johnson complained to the Lords of Trade that the traders' treatment of the Native Americans and one another was so bad that the natives now trusted no one. The traders were accusing one another of the most despicable acts, many of which were true. The murder and robbery of rival trading companies was common. All the traders were using rum at an alarming rate, which the Native Americans were referring to as "English milk," regardless of the restrictions or penalties. (Ibid., p. 969.)

In an effort to stop the chaos that had become the hallmark of the trade, Johnson suggested that the traders be restricted to certain posts, rather than being allowed free access to the interior. (Ibid., p. 966.) The recommendation was also made that inspectors be stationed at these posts to enforce all trade regulations.[60] While this plan was good in theory, like so many others, it was impractical in application. There were too many ways that an ingenious trader could avoid detection or inspection — failing that, there was always bribery.[61]

The Native Americans themselves were also a problem. They depended on the traders coming to them, as they had done under the French rule. For many years their needs had been serviced by traders who had wintered in or near their villages. They were now unwilling to travel hundreds of miles, in some cases, to trade at the posts. The Native Americans also complained that these long journeys interfered with the amount of furs that they were able to harvest, and left their villages vulnerable to the raids of their enemies. (Ibid., p. 965.)

---

[60] Hay, *Michigan Pioneer*, Vol. XI, p. 490.
[61] O'Callaghan, *DRCHSNY*, Vol. VII, p. 853.

An alternate plan was recommended, that inspectors be sent into the wilderness to regulate the trade.[62] This plan was as foolhardy as expecting the traders to submit to inspections or to remain at the posts. Once beyond the bounds of the frontier a man could disappear without a trace. When the plan was implemented, those inspectors who ventured into the interior found it easier, and more lucrative, to accept or extract bribes from the traders than to enforce regulations.[63]

The crown found that while it might be possible to regulate the trade with a combination of any or all of these plans, the expense was staggering. Rather than proving to be a boon that would fill the royal treasury, the western fur trade was proving to be an expensive burden. The costs of staffing the Department of Indian Affairs with inspectors, translators and gifts to appease the natives, were far out-stripping the revenues to be gained.

It was finally decided that there was no need to pay two groups to do the same job. The military had to be at the western posts to guard the frontier. Logically they should also be in charge of regulating the trade. In this way only a small force of Indian agents would be needed to assist the post commanders.

This system was very similar to that of the French regime. The post commanders had the power to enforce all regulations as well as the power to sign all treaties with the native tribes for trade or military reasons in the name of the king. This plan proved to be as unworkable for the English as it had been for the French. There was just too much territory to control and too many groups with diverse interests to be appeased. Added to this were the problems of over-ambitious officers, conflicting regulations and a constant lack of funds.

Officers often sold exclusive rights to a particular person for trade in a given area. An example is the case of Alexander Henry, who was given the exclusive rights to the Lake Superior

---

[62] Hay, *Michigan Pioneer*, Vol. XI, p. 491.
[63] O'Callaghan, *DRCHSNY*, Vol. VII, p. 974.

country by the commander of Michilimackinac.[64] Other officers, such as Robert Rogers, took advantage of their position to outfit expeditions of their own. Rogers sent an expedition in search of the headwaters of the Mississippi with the dual purpose of trading for furs. His plan was to build a distillery near the headwaters of the Mississippi to reduce the transportation cost of liquor for the trade. This could have proved to be a very lucrative establishment for its owners, one of whom was to be Rogers, if it had been completed. Rogers' arrest on trumped-up charges and his removal from the post ended his plan.[65] The English found, like the French before them, that while the idea of allowing the military to regulate the bulk of the trade was far from a perfect solution, it was better than no regulation at all.

This put the British commanders in an even more unworkable position than it had the French. The military commander or governor of a post was forced to answer to two authorities. As an officer he must answer to his direct military superior, but at the same time, as the king's representative among the Native Americans, he was subject to the rules and regulations of the Superintendent of Indian Affairs. These two departments being at odds with one another, more often than not placed the post commander in an untenable position as to the best course to follow in dealing with the Native Americans. Orders from the military establishment required restraint in the amount and types of gifts to be given to the Native Americans. At the same time the Indian Department ordered the lavish amounts and a wide array of gifts to be given. The Indian Department set the regulations, but the military provided the funds. The officers often found themselves relying on their personal funds to fulfill the promises made by the Indian Department. In these cases the officer was to submit a voucher

---

[64] Henry, *Voyages*, p. 182.

[65] John Parker, "New Light on Jonathan Carver," *The American Magazine and Historical Chronicle* (Vol. 2, No. 1, Spring-Summer, 1986), p. 16.

to the government for reimbursement. Such requests for expenses were often denied.

These were some of the major problems facing those who attempted to regulate the fur trade and administer the newly claimed territories of the Great Lakes.

HUDSON'S BAY COMPANY

For close to 100 years Hudson's Bay Company sat quietly beside its bay, gathering strength and waiting for the time when it could spread across the land. "The Company" was not plagued with many of the problems that were faced by those to the south in the years before 1763. This was due, in part, to their location. In the far north, where goods and furs could only be taken out by ship, and only company ships could dock, smuggling was unknown.[66] The isolation of the Company posts, and lack of possible military assistance, forced the Company to deal in a fair manner with the natives. With the constant threat of French incursion, the Company could not risk alienating the native population. Many times in the barren wastes of the far north, the Native American hunters were all that stood between the men of the Hudson's Bay Company and starvation.

With a royal charter that made it not only a monopoly but also a sovereign governing body answerable only to its board of directors and the king, the Hudson's Bay Company had all the makings of a colony. The poor land and isolation of the bay limited it to a mere fur gathering operation. Requiring only enough land for a few posts, the company placed no great demands on the native population for land use. The Company was able to supply all the needs of its native customers by direct importation or home manufacture. Trade goods such as axes, chisels, traps and other iron goods were manufactured on

---

[66] Harold A. Innis, *The Fur Trade in Canada* (Toronto, Canada: University of Toronto Press, 1956), 127-128.

site to the specifications of the native hunters. Those goods that could not be manufactured easily at the posts were brought from England once a year by ship.

With this background and power it would seem that the Hudson's Bay Company would be the dominating force after 1760. This was not the case however. After the end of the Seven Years' War, the Company found itself fighting for its very survival. This time the challenge was not from hostile natives or foreign power but from their own countrymen and government. The effect of this struggle would be felt throughout the Northwest but most particularly in the Great Lakes.

With the end of the Seven Years' War, the Hudson's Bay Company began to expand southward with the objective of controlling the rich fur trade to the west. This would mean that they would have to take control of the lakes as well. At the same time, hundreds of would-be traders were flooding into the country to the west of the Great Lakes, to reap the rich harvest of furs. It was inevitable that these two forces would clash, despite all government regulation or control.

As the Company sent its traders south and west over the "Height of Land" which divided the watershed of the Great Lakes from that of Hudson's Bay, they found the country flooded with independent traders. The first reaction of the Company was contempt. These newcomers would be swept aside by the superior power and ability of the Company, with its better organization and finances. This did not happen. The independents had neither the organization nor the financial power of the great Hudson's Bay Company, but the independents did not have the hundreds of employees and their dependents to support, nor did they have the expenses of established posts to maintain. The Company moved at a slow methodical pace, securing trading rights as they went, either through direct contact or through their native middlemen.

The newcomers, on the other hand, moved swiftly from place to place. Their only concern was the gathering of the largest amount of furs as quickly as possible. Where the company could send a hundred canoes, the independents could only send ten, but even this numerical advantage worked against the Company. Large numbers of men had to be fed and supplied, if the faster moving, smaller groups of independents had gotten to the trading grounds first, the much needed supplies of food, as well as pelts, had already been traded for and the independents had moved on. (Ibid, p. 138.) Where the Company could offer better goods, the independents could offer cheaper goods at lower prices. The result of this competition was war. It was once again a seller's market. The Native Americans had gained a semblance of the old economic control that they had held during the late war.

At first it was a war of words. Each side called the other liars and cheats, which was often the truth. All the traders, Company and independent, were guilty of using such improper business practices as lightweight scales and gunpowder mixed with sand.[67] It did not take long before this war of words became a war of bullets. The Northwest was a vast uncharted territory in which canoe brigades could disappear without a trace. Brigades were ambushed and plundered by their competition with little fear of discovery. (Ibid.) Native Americans were bribed to murder of plunder traders for a keg of rum. It was at this point that the Company had the upper hand, with its ready-made army of employees and middlemen. The independents, in their mad scramble for a share of the market, were as likely to attack one another as the Company.

With the trade once again a seller's market, the Native Americans were the only true beneficiaries of this economic guerrilla warfare. The native hunter could once again sell his pelts to the highest bidder, playing one side of against the other. They had been given control again through unbridled competition between an unlimited set of buyers. The Native Americans were free, once again, to set the standards of quality

---

[67] O'Callaghan, *DRCHSNY*, Vol. VII, p. 961.

and quantity for which they were willing to trade.[68] They could force both sides to trade on their terms with the mere threat of taking their business elsewhere. The natives would buy their goods on credit from one trader in the fall, the furs that were to pay for these goods were often then traded to a competitor in the spring. (Ibid.) This was especially true if the second trader was willing to trade for rum. As we shall see, the liquor trade was to prove ruinous to the Native American and his culture. Trading on credit was to prove to be the ruin of many a trader, who had purchased the goods on credit himself. The traders found themselves at the mercy of the Native Americans, who neither understood nor cared about the economics of the trade.

This ruinous situation could not continue for long. As the crushing numbers of the Company began to take a toll on the independents, and attempts at regulation by the government became stronger, the independents found it necessary to band together. The growing tensions between the colonies and the mother country added to this need for unity. Petty differences were soon forgotten in a need for stronger alliances; it was better to get a smaller share of the market then none at all.

As the American Revolution broke out in the East, a change was forced on the fur trade of the West. This, along with the economic pressures that had risen in the trade, resulted in the thinning of the number of independents. Those resourceful enough to survive the first years of the trade wars began to band together in uneasy trade alliances or confederations. The result of one such ad hoc partnership was the formation of the Northwest Company in 1783. By banding together these traders were able to field a force equal to that of the Hudson's Bay Company in finances and manpower. (Ibid.) In a short time these two fur-trading giants were able to force out almost all the competition.

The battle lines were drawn; it was a winner-take-all situation. The winner would have a virtual empire stretching from Hudson's Bay to the shores of the Ohio; from the Atlantic

---

[68] Askin Papers, p. 283.

Ocean to the Rocky Mountains. At the heart of this empire would be the crossroads of the Great Lakes.

The Nor'westers, or "the Competition," as the new company became known, had control of the key points in the lakes and the St. Lawrence River valley. This gave them the decided advantage of a longer shipping season. The short summers and long frozen winter gave The Company only a limited time to bring in supplies and send out furs. The Company, however, had the advantage of long established trade with tribes of the northern plains and a well-established middleman system with the Cree, whom they referred to as their "home guard."[69]

In an effort to establish supremacy over the western trade, both companies raced across Canada to establish posts on the west coast. The Competition hoped to close off the Company, and the Company to establish a second source of supply with a longer shipping season. The struggle for control would not be settled until the two giants finally merged in the 1800's.

GOVERNMENT POLICY

The policies of the fur trade during the period of British occupation were inefficient at best and chaotic at the worst. The division of power between the various governmental departments overlapped to the point of confusion and contradiction. The ideas of revenue and regulation were at constant odds with one another. Maximizing revenue meant deregulation of the fur trade. Efficient regulation of the trade meant the expenditure of massive amounts of money. These two tenets of government were irreconcilable during the eighteenth century.

The one constant was the idea of open trade, open to any English subject for the cost of a license. How open was "open trade," really was a matter of personal definition. In theory anyone with the proper license could trade anywhere in the

---

[69] Arthur J. Ray, *Indians in the Fur Trade*, pp. 59-61.

territory. As in the case of the Hudson's Bay Company, however, vast areas were handed over to groups of investors as a private preserve. The sole right to a territory could be given, for a price, by the commander of a post governing the area.[70] In these cases the individuals were following in the footsteps of the French traders who bribed post commanders and officials for the right to trade in a given area.

While neither Alexander Henry, nor any other trader directly stated that they bribed an officer for the privilege of trading in a prime location, their actions would suggest that such activities occurred. Corruption was commonplace in the British army. Officers were not promoted by the ability to command but rather by their ability to pay. Military careers were seen as a way for second sons to make their fortune. It was also a stepping-stone into the world of politics and a seat in parliament. The contention was that those who were born to privilege were born to lead. While many of the officers took seriously their responsibility to king and country, others saw it as an opportunity for self-enrichment. Quartermasters would sell rations and goods destined for the frontier garrisons to local traders and then buy them back again at a highly inflated price, for a share of the profits.[71] In many cases a "blind eye" was turned toward this type of activity, unless it interfered with the war. Many of the British officers after 1763 were directly involved in the trade. Captain James Rutherford and others used traders such as James Sterling of Detroit as their agents in the sale of goods. Traders were not above hiring enlisted men to act as collection agents for them, although this activity was strictly forbidden by military law.[72]

Corruption was not limited to the military alone. Government agents such as inspectors and interpreters for the Department of Indian Affairs were often involved in private dealings with traders and natives.[73] Such prominent men as

---

[70] Henry, *Voyages*, p. 192.
[71] Sterling's Letter Book, p. 25.
[72] Amherst Papers, 70:185.
[73] Hay, *Michigan Pioneer*, Vol. XI, pp. 565-566.

George Croghan, Guy Johnson and even Sir William Johnson were not above using their positions for personal gain. This corruption was common throughout eighteenth-century society, but was rampant on the frontier due to the lack of uniform regulation and authority.

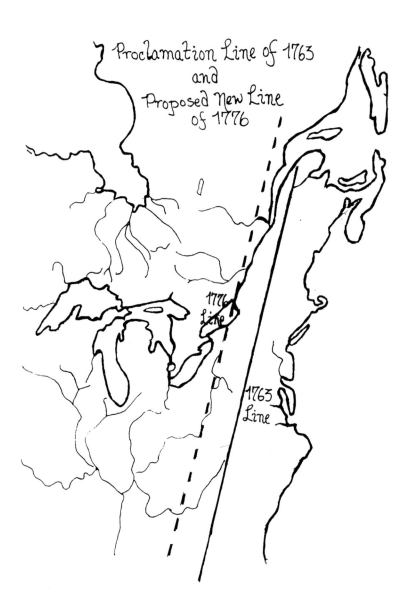

Proclamation Line of 1763
and
Proposed New Line
of 1776

1776 Line

1763 Line

CHAPTER 7

The Fur Trade and Its Effects On Native American Culture

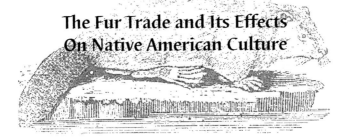

When the Native Americans accepted the first trinkets from the Europeans, forces were set in motion that would change their world for all time. The colonization of North America by the Europeans would be marked by contact, conflict and accommodation. All of these actions would result in a changing of Native American culture. Alterations would take place on every level of society tribal structure, living habits and religion. These modifications would shake the culture of the Native Americans to its very foundation.

The long-established routes of trade became the highways for new and miraculous goods that flowed from the European settlements. The system of exchange that passed goods from hand to hand sent such things as steel knives, copper kettles, iron awls and glass beads inland far ahead of the Europeans themselves. What started as a slow trickle of trade goods soon became a torrent to fill an insatiable demand. Iron and steel tools quickly replaced those of stone, wood and bone. Cloth began to replace leather for clothing and wool blankets replaced furs for bedding and winter wear. These were all magical items far beyond the ability of the native people to manufacture on their own. The native people were discriminating buyers, however, and it was not long before they began to demand goods of a particular type, size or color, and would accept no others. This new market was a buyer's market, in which the quality and quantity of goods was to be set by the native people. The Hudson's Bay Company was soon to find that axes of a certain size and weight were all that the Native Americans would accept in trade, all others would be left to rust on the shelves. The same was true of muskets. Only those bearing a serpentine side plate and stamped with a sitting fox on the barrel and lock were seen as having value to the native hunters, regardless of quality. In a letter to one of his suppliers James Sterling of Fort Detroit complained:

> *"Thirty-one of the French blankets which are very good and only wanting a row of capital letters ranging close along the inside of one of the stripes of each blanket, the stripes are also most commonly blue than black but never ought to exceed a full inch or an inch and a half in breath.*
>
> *I understand by Mr. Posteous that there is in the cargo at Niagara a quantity of English blankets with red stripes; I am surprised that such things are sent, they will not sell here in seven years."*[72]

This entry, along with others in Sterling's letter book show to what degree the Native Americans were able to control the commodities that were offered for trade. In another entry Sterling comments that blue cloth was preferred for leggings. The preferences of the native people were so strong that they could even affect trade half a world away. One of the most sought after commodities was vermilion, but not just any grade of vermilion would do. Only Chinese vermilion was deemed acceptable. Beads were imported from Venice and calico from India, all of which had to be made to the specifications of the customers.

Some items had even taken on a religious significance, or at the very least were influenced by Native American religion. In the case of the trade musket, the serpentine side plate and the sitting fox could be seen as having a great deal of significance beyond being purely ornamental. The Native American people were spiritualists. They believed that all things, animate and inanimate, had a spirit. To create a picture or image of a creature or object was to summon that

---

[72] Eccles, *Canadian Frontier*, p. 31.

spirit's aid. The great power of the gun was enhanced by summoning the cunning of the fox and the speed and accuracy of the snake to the aid of the hunter. The bow and arrow was by far a superior weapon in war to the flintlock musket, but the musket's ability to kill almost instantaneously, with the power of smoke and fire and the roar of thunder, made it a powerful hunting tool. It could summon up the very forces of nature to aid a man in his never-ending quest for food.

The copper kettle, a common cooking utensil in any European home, took on a new meaning to the people of the Great Lakes. Copper was seen to be of great value among many native people. To them it represented the scales of the great turtle, on whose back the Earth rode. The kettles themselves were of very little value to a semi-nomadic people who must carry everything they owned with them. Without a beast of burden other than the dog, any extra weight was an unneeded burden. The copper of the kettle, however, could be cut up and made into highly prized ornaments, such as ear and nose rings, armbands and bracelets. By the end of the eighteenth century the Native Americans in the Great Lakes country had even begun to use horses as beasts of burden, if not for riding. There is also evidence that they were using batteaux along with the more traditional canoe, as witnessed by Major Gladwin in the siege of Detroit.

All of these adaptations, and many more, had a long-lasting effect on the Native Americans. On a very base level the economy of the Native Americans had changed from that of hunter-gatherer or hunter-gatherer-farmer to that of hunter-gatherer-consumer, and consumer on an ever-growing scale. The animals that once were a resource unto themselves, to be harvested as the need arose, were now a medium of exchange. This new way of living required a change in the basic thinking of the native religion. All human action requires justification, even if that justification required a change in one's basic beliefs. So it was with the Native Americans and the harvesting of beaver for their pelts alone.

To justify their actions the Native Americans went, like most people, to their religion. According to Native American mythology, the beaver was like man. The beaver could walk upright and speak. The beaver became arrogant and began to think himself as great as Gichi Manitou, the Great Creator. Of all the creatures in the world only the beaver could create his own world. The Gichi Manitou punished the beaver for his pride and took away his power of speech and made him walk on all fours. It was an easy stretch of logic for the native people to justify their killing the beaver by saying: "we are doing the Manitou's bidding by declaring war on the beaver and punishing him for his pride." This is just one of the many changes that the Native American religion would undergo after contact with the Europeans.

SOCIAL STRUCTURE

Through the slow and continuous mechanism of contact and trade, the Native Americans of the Great Lakes found their lives changing. These changes affected the very fabric of their society and their relationship with other tribal groups. Over the centuries prior to contact, the native peoples had developed a trade network, as mentioned above, by which goods could be passed from one end of the continent to the other and back again. This network was made up of a series of middlemen, all of whom jealously guarded their position in the chain of trade. With the coming of European trade goods the position of these middlemen became even more substantial. Through this system the controlling tribes were able to dominate the region in which they lived as well as the trade. Tribal groups such as the Ottawa were able to extend their trade network far to the west and north, forming alliances with new trading partners. These alliances often went beyond the bounds of mere trading partnerships, and included war alliances as well as some hunting rights. In this way the middlemen were able to form loose trade confederations, with themselves at the head. (Ibid., p. 125.) Control of these confederations could be maintained through the flow of goods in a form of economic blackmail. At first, most of the goods traded were of a second-hand nature, either used or inferior to those that the middlemen received in trade from the Europeans directly. The middlemen could control the flow of goods to those outside the trade network through exclusion.[73] This control of goods gave the members of the trading confederacy military dominance, particularly after the introduction of firearms. This type of military superiority allowed a tribe to increase its territory through warfare; thus expanding their ability to harvest even more furs for trade as well as increasing their control over their neighbors.[74]

This major shift in political and economic structure of the tribe would in turn cause a shift in tribal structure, politics and relationships. The political orientation of the tribal groups began to change. Now, along with war and peace councils, trade councils were held. The organization of trading parties was now as important to the survival of the group as a well-organized hunting or war party. A successful trade leader, one who had proven his ability to drive a hard bargain, was as important as a strong war leader or negotiator in times of peace. Once a leader had made a name for himself, he would call for volunteers for a trading party. Each member would be allowed to trade a set amount of furs for himself. The leader of the party would handle the bulk of the trade negotiations. Prior to the party's departure, each member of the group would advise the leader of his wants and needs. A tally would be made of each member's furs and goods needed. It was up to the leader to strike the best deal possible for those who had entrusted him with their furs. If the leader were to fail or be cheated he would never again lead another such party. A successful leader, through shrewd

---

[73] O'Callaghan, *DRCHSNY*, Vol. IX, p. 673.
[74] Kinietz, *Indians of the Great Lakes*, p. 46.

trading, could enhance his own personal wealth and position in the tribe. Tribal leaders were now chosen on their abilities as traders as well as bravery and wisdom. (Ibid.) In Algonkin society the personal wealth of an individual, and his ability or willingness to give that wealth away, was as important as bravery. By giving gifts, a leader or potential leader demonstrated his willingness to care for others. In a society that had the family structure as its basic unit of government, this willingness to provide for others was most important. (Ibid., pp. 53-56.)

A tribal leader could not enforce his will over other members of the group. He must influence them by his ability to provide for the good of all, be it in war or peace. This lack of absolute power would always be a strong point of contention between the native people and the Europeans. The basis of Native American society was one of communalism. That is to say that the individual is equal to the whole. This concept works well in a hunter-gatherer society, but not quite as well in a consumer-oriented one. So as the society of the native people shifted from that of hunter-gatherer to hunter-consumer the focus of the society began to shift. The individual now became greater than the whole and personal wealth and greed became a part of the society. A leader or person of wealth could now dispense his favors to gain more influence and personal power not just for the good of the whole group.[75]

The clan system, which was the basic extended family of all Native Americans, was also forced to change. Among the Algonkin people, lines of descent and clan relationship were passed from the father. When more extensive contact occurred with the Europeans, and interracial relationships took place, children were born who had no clan. A person's position within the tribe was decided by their clan and their position within that clan. As a result, those born without a

---

[75] Jennifer S.H. Brown, *Strangers in Blood: Fur Trade Company Families in Indian Country* (Vancouver, Canada: University of British Columbia Press, 1940), p. 25.

clan were outside the tribal structure and had no place within the society. This became a serious problem among a people who counted their power in martial terms. Anyone not a member of the tribe could not be counted on for the defense of the group. As non-members of the tribe a person of mixed-blood had no rights under tribal law. In response to this serious problem the clan structure changed. Among the Algonkin people, two new clans were created and added to the traditional ones: the Eagle clan for those of French descent and the Lion for those of English descent.[76]

These family ties worked to the advantage of those associated with a member of the new clans when trading, particularly if the father was a local trader. Such a man would be expected to show "pity" to his "wife's" family. As a result, while he could expect to be give exclusive rights to the family trade, he could also expect to be smothered with a parade of poor relatives who would be looking for gifts. It was most often the sons and daughters of these men who drew the full advantage of their dual heritage. While they may have been looked down upon as half-breeds by white society, they were indispensable as interpreters and negotiators to the leaders of both European and native groups.

The fur trade also caused changes in the everyday activities and seasonal way of life of the Great Lakes people. Hunting had changed from a mere source of food gathering to a form of employment. This led to a breakdown of the traditional hunting territorial system within which the tribe had functioned. According to tribal tradition, each hunter was allowed a certain territory, the boundaries of which were well known within the group. To cross into another's hunting ground meant that the violator would have to give up a percentage of his kill as tribute to the owner. (Ibid., p. 253.) To survive, however, a hunter had to keep as much of his catch as he could. As hunting pressure increased, such traditions began to be violated or ignored. This in turn

---

[76] Warren, *Ojibway People*, p. 252.

increased tension within the tribal group and lead to an increase in personal disputes and a breakdown of the social structure. For those groups that had become more settled and dependent on agriculture, the increased time spent hunting and trading meant less manpower at the critical times of harvesting and planting. While farming may have been considered women's work, everyone was needed in the spring and fall to clear fields and harvest crops. These had now become the times when the men were far afield either trading of trapping. In turn, much-needed food supplies could be endangered by this lack of manpower.

As the trade began to move beyond the Great Lakes after 1763, some of the tribes began to produce food for trade. The British employed native hunters to supply meat for the garrisons of forts, such as Detroit.[77] Crops such as corn and wild rice, which formerly had been used as a winter food supply by the tribes, were now traded to the garrisons. Fish, which could be found in great abundance in the lakes, were smoked or dried and also traded to the garrisons. The result was that often the tribes would find themselves running short of food in the winter months. They would then have to beg the garrisons or depend on gifts of food from the military or traders. Most of what they were given was in the form of salted meat and flour, which had been intended for the fort's rations.[78]

There was also a change in the structure of the family and how members of the family interacted. The women, who had spent much of their time during the winter making the clothing and other necessities for their families, were employed scraping and preparing furs for market. The clothing that the women would have made was now purchased from the trader, or at least the materials such as wool and cotton cloth were added to the list of trade necessities. The fur hides that once would have made up a

---

[77] Armour & Widder, *Crossroads*, p. 20.
[78] Jacobs, *Wilderness Politics*, p. 46.

large part of the needed raw materials were now needed to fulfill the debt to the European trader. Women were no longer only keepers of the home and hearth, but now a part of the vast expanding work force of the fur trade.

RELIGION

The fur trade brought on changes in the traditional belief system of the native people of the Great Lakes. Many of the traditional stories and beliefs, such as the one of the beaver mentioned above, were changed or altogether dropped from the native belief system. Once the native belief system had changed enough for the justification of the fur trade, it was an easy thing for the native people to exchange or at least adopt that of the Europeans. Through the work of French missionaries, who both preceded and followed the traders, native beliefs were challenged and oft times erased. If the Europeans as a whole were perceived to be gifted with great magical powers, then the missionaries, such as the Jesuits, were seen to be great shamans. We know from a study of *Jesuit Relations* that the Jesuit fathers were seen as the doers of great things. As mentioned earlier, the Native American belief system was based on spiritualism and the mystical gifts that these spirits could bestow on people. It was not difficult for the Jesuits, whether by accident or design, to manipulate this simple system for their own uses. Many of the natives were converted to Catholicism, which was to the advantage of the French during their rule of the Northwest. It did not take long until the natives were caught in a religious conflict among themselves. Tribes such as the Mohawk of western New York found themselves divided into two groups: those who followed the old ways and those who followed the teachings of the "Black Robes." It was not long before these two groups split apart. Those who followed the teachings of the new religion moved north to the shores of the St.

Lawrence, forming "praying towns" under the watchful eye of the Jesuits.

Many peoples were divided by the new religion. Most did not divide themselves as easily or as quietly as the Mohawks. In the case of the Iroquois, religious division would make them easy prey for their blood enemies, the Huron. The end result would be the breakup of the Huron people and an end to their dominance of the fur trade in the eastern Lake country.

With the takeover of the western trade by the English, the Roman Catholic religion was all but banned in the Great Lakes until the Quebec Act of 1774.[79] Many of those native people who followed this belief found themselves without religious leaders and nothing to fill this void. The English did little or nothing to fill the void. They were more interested in the production of furs rather than the saving of souls.

WARFARE

Warfare before the coming of Europeans was a matter of survival on a personal level. It is a fact of nature that only so many animals can live on a given amount of land, and in turn only so many people can live off of that number of animals. That makes anyone who is not related to you in some way an enemy. In most Native American languages there is no word for friend. There are many designations for family members, such as father, mother, sister, brother, aunt, uncle, grand-father and grandmother, all of which show the degree and type of relationship between members of a group. But the abstract idea of an unrelated individual does not exist. Therefore any unrelated individual is an enemy. As such anyone not related to you is not of the "People;" an almost universal term used in one form or another by all Native Americans to designate themselves from all those around

---

[79] Martin, *Keepers*, p. 65.

them. Anyone who is not of your group of people, or at least allied with you, is an enemy by virtue of their very existence. If they hunt or forage in or near your territory, these people are taking food from your mouth and thereby threatening your life.

This very simple code was the basis of life in a hunter-gatherer society. Warfare was a necessary part of their way of life, but not warfare as we define it today. Warfare in pre-Columbian America was more a matter of hit-and-run raids conducted by small groups upon one another. Most often the objects of these raids were foodstuffs such as corn or rice, or perhaps the kidnapping of individuals to offset losses in their own population. Whichever was the case, bloodshed was usually kept to a minimum. Major conflicts over territory were the exception to this rule. If one group's population had far exceeded the ability of the land to support it, or if major migration was forced upon a group, then large-scale warfare may have followed. Smaller territorial disputes could be settled by a game of Indian lacrosse or *begadaway*. The Algonkin word *begadaway* can be literally translated to "the little brother of war." It was not uncommon for major injuries or even deaths to occur during one of these games. Major wars of extermination, which are common in western European culture, did not occur prior to European contact. Such wars were not of use in Native American culture. It was far better to drive an enemy from the territory, even in the case of mass migrations to new territory. Total elimination of an enemy was not seen as necessary.

After the arrival of Europeans, and the total shifting of the economic base of the Native Americans, warfare changed. The control of territory now meant a greater harvest of furs. In many cases once the controlled hunting ground of a group, such as the Iroquois, had been hunted out. Open warfare for control of expanded territory, or of the trade within that territory, became a necessity for the group to keep up their new standard of living. In the inter-tribal fur trade, competition was dealt with swiftly and viciously. Such were the cases of the Huron/Iroquois "beaver wars" of the seventeenth century, and the Ottawa/Fox wars of the eighteenth century. Warfare was now a matter of economic survival. Animals now were not just a food source but were also "money," a medium of exchange. What they could bring in the way of manufactured goods determined a whole new lifestyle for the native people. Greed had entered the picture in a major way for these people, whose existence previously had been one of communal sharing and semi-coexistence.

THE NATIVE AMERICAN AS A CONSUMER

Along with the breakdown of tribal society and structure came the need for more consumer goods. The very basis of the fur trade was the natives' need and dependence on the Europeans for goods that they could not manufacture themselves. By the end of the Seven Years' War this dependence had grown to such a point that the Native Americans could no longer live without these goods. (Ibid., p. 62.) This was a dependence that the English not only relied on but fostered to an even greater extent than the French had.[80] The English were well aware of the usefulness of this dependence and needed the land that was now occupied by the Native Americans. They also realized that to attempt to take that land by force would be foolhardy. Rather it was easier to convert the native into a semblance of a European, or failing that, make the native people so dependent upon them that they could not economically afford to resist encroachment.

The introduction of firearms to the Native Americans was to change their way of life more than any other trade item. The advantage the gun had over the traditional weapons of war was more psychological then physical, but its use by the Native American fostered an ever-growing reliance on the

---

[80] O'Callaghan, *DRCHSNY*, Vol. XII, p. 550.

European supplier. The traditional bow and arrow was far superior in rate of fire over the muzzle-loading flintlock musket. It was in the all important area of the hunt that the musket came into its own. A hunter might fire as many as five or six arrows into a moose before downing the animal, which could still travel for more than a mile before dying. A single well-placed musket ball could stop it within moments of being hit. The difference in a bad winter could mean life or death to an exhausted hunter. The calories saved by not having to pursue a wounded animal through deep snow or heavy cover meant a gain in the face of harsh winter survival. Game could now be taken more efficiently and safely than in the past. Once the native hunter had adopted this new form of game getting, however, he was forever dependent on the European for his supply of ammunition as well as repairs or replacement of the weapon.

In warfare the gun was great magic. It harnessed the power of thunder and lightning. The psychological effect on an enemy could be devastating, especially in the first encounter. When the tribes of the Great Lakes had acquired the gun they proceeded to press their advantage over their enemies. This advantage allowed the Chippewa to drive out their traditional enemies, the Lakota, from the Upper Peninsula of Michigan and on to the plains. It also allowed the Ottawa to press their position of middleman to the west. Control over the supply of guns, powder and lead gave any tribe an economic hold over its neighbors and trading partners, much as the Europeans had over them.

The natives became totally dependent on the Europeans, whether they were primary consumers or middlemen, for supply and repair of all firearms. The result of this dilemma was that any Native American in possession of a firearm must travel to a European to have it worked on or replaced. In answer to this and to increase trade as well as ties of dependence, the French, as well as the Hudson's Bay Company, were in the habit of providing gunsmiths at their posts.[81] Although Edmond Atkin had pointed this out in his report to the Lords of Trade and Plantations in 1755, it took a number of years for the British to adopt this same policy.[82] The main fear of the English was that the natives would revolt again if they were provided with reliable firearms.[83]

By the time of the British occupation of the Great Lakes, the tribes were so dependent on the gun that they could not live without it. This in turn gave the English a hold on the Native Americans that the French had only fostered. With no one to supply them with powder and lead except the English, the natives were now totally dependent on them for their way of life. It was this dependency, more than anything else, that would lead to the uprising of the 1760's.

It is a well recorded fact that the Native Americans, of this time period, never fully understood the finer points of using a firearm. When in possession of powder the Native Americans were most wasteful, discharging it for any reason and often over-charging the weapon when using it. As a result the amount of powder that would have been more than sufficient for a European was far from adequate for a Native American. This was a problem that the British military never understood.[84] To the native hunter it was the loud blast and flash of flame, as much as the musket ball, that made the gun such a magical weapon.

While the gun made the taking of big game much more efficient, it was the introduction of the steel-jaw trap, by the British after 1760, that was to improve the fur trade itself. The traditional method of taking beaver was to chop a hole into an ice-bound lodge during the winter, or to set a snare. Both of these methods were inefficient and wasteful, as they often either failed to work or killed both young and old beavers alike. The steel-jaw trap proved to be a more effective and less dangerous method of taking beaver as well as other fur-

---

[81] Quimby, *Culture*, p. 150.
[82] O'Callaghan, *DRCHSNY*, Vol. V, p. 958.
[83] Eccles, *Canadian Frontier*, p. 125.
[84] Amherst Papers, 7:179.

bearing animals. This new method of trapping allowed for an increase in the killing of mature beaver and contributed to a more rapid decline in the beaver population.

On a more personal basis of consumption, the use of cloth in the manufacture of clothing added yet another strand in the web of dependence. The hides and furs that had once made up the Native Americans' clothing were now needed for trade. Cloth not only proved to be a logical substitute but was a more practical material. Clothing made of only leather, while highly durable, was of little comfort in inclement weather. Clothing made of wool or cotton proved to be more functional and could be made with much less preparation. Once again, however, the Native American could not produce this and was dependent on the European for a constant supply.

As the fur trade and its participants grew more sophisticated, so did the medium of exchange. It did not take long before the Native American began to supply necessary goods and services to the Europeans for money. As has been mentioned above, the natives were willing to perform such services as boatmen, mercenaries, guides, interpreters, laborers, or even farmers for a price. Many times that price was far higher than that of their European counterparts. During the Seven Years' War Native American auxiliaries, used by both the French and the British, cost twice as much as European troops in coin as well as gifts. The value that the European placed on these strange pieces of metal was not lost on the native consumer.[85] This practice of working for a set fee was to become yet another step in the erosion of native culture and traditional values.

---

[85] Innis, *Fur Trade*, pp. 411-412.

LAND AND OWNERSHIP

Once the Native American's society and culture was corrupted, his food supply decimated, and his total dependence on the European assured, nothing was left but the land. To a Native American, ownership of land was a vague concept at best. The idea of permanent occupation of an area was foreign to the comprehension of nomadic or semi-nomadic people. Land was a resource to be used as any other, but was seen as being fluid, like the waters of the Lakes. One could claim usage of it but never possession. Land could not be transported, nor could an individual take all that was needed from a single spot; even a hunter had to travel to find more game to provide for his needs. Areas could be set aside for the harvesting of game or the planting of crops, but this concept did not carry with it the implication of ownership. It was, rather, a concept of mere occupancy. All territory claimed by a given tribe was seen as being held in common. The amount of land that a group held under its control dictated its food supply. The larger the tribal group, the larger the amount of territory it must control. As the tribal group became less important and the needs of the individual grew more important during the time of the fur trade, so did the Native Americans' ideas regarding land and ownership change.

At first the native people could see the benefit of ceding a few acres of land to the Europeans for a trading post. Having the traders in their territory was of benefit to both parties; also, the traders were willing to pay for the privilege with gifts. As control over the trade increased and the need for military presence became greater, so did the need for more land. This too was of benefit to both parties, as it increased the amount of trade as well as gifts. With the increased size of the posts and military garrisons came the civilians and need for even more land. Now the idea of land ownership became clouded.

An individual might cede his rights to a piece of land to another person for a period of time, but to the native people this only implied land usage, not ownership. To the European, however, such dealings were seen as permanent and binding. As these land claims by the Europeans increased and settlements expanded, the pressure for adequate hunting land grew. The added pressure on the environment forced more and more changes in Native American society and life. Many tribal groups found it impossible to remain in their traditional lands and maintain any semblance of their own culture. Those who refused to give over to the European way of living were forced to move to the north and west in an attempt to keep the Europeans at arm's length. While they were forever tied to the Europeans, they would still try to keep their own identity and culture as long as they could. This was a battle that they were doomed to lose. By the end of British occupation of the Northwest, the Native American culture of the Great Lakes had become but a shadow of what it once had been.

CHAPTER 8

The Use and Abuse of Liquor in the Fur Trade

Nothing, with the possible exception of disease, had a more devastating effect on the Native Americans than alcohol. Its use in the fur trade was widely renounced by everyone involved; at the same time it was a necessity of life in the trade. All attempts to regulate or ban the use of liquor proved useless. Its effects on the Native Americans are well recorded. The use of strong drink in Native American society was unheard of, in the Great Lakes, prior to the coming of the Europeans. The introduction of alcohol had a negative effect on native society as a whole.[86]

When and where the first Native American drank the first European liquor is not known, nor were its effects ever recorded. What is known is that wherever European and native people met, liquor was consumed and the effects on the natives were ruinous. European liquor, English rum and French brandy in particular, were so shocking to the Native American that anyone under its influence was forgiven all crimes he had committed while intoxicated. The excuse given for such crimes was that it had been the spirit of the liquor, not the person, that had committed the act. Under the influence of alcohol, any crime imaginable could be and was committed. Murder and rape were commonplace on drunken binges. Even after seeing the results of their drunken behavior the natives would ask for more liquor. (Ibid.)

---

86 Warren, *Ojibway People*, p. 190.

Under the French rule only enough liquor was to be taken by traders for personal use; the limit was one pint per day per man.[87] This was often ignored by the traders. They would smuggle large quantities of brandy upriver before leaving for the frontier, then retrieve it after the canoes had passed inspection. (Ibid., p. 7.) The traders had learned early that the Native Americans would quickly trade an entire winter's catch of furs for a few barrels of cheap brandy. Both the Jesuit missionaries and the tribal leaders begged the government of New France to stop the trade in liquor. It would appear once the market was opened there was no way of stopping the flow.

By the outbreak of the Seven Years' War, the French government had stopped trying to ban the use of alcohol as a trade item. Licensed traders were allowed to carry twenty gallons of brandy for trade per canoe. Even with this lenient policy, smuggling was still a problem.[88]

By 1760 the use of liquor as a medium of trade had reached such great proportions that the British general, Sir Jeffrey Amherst, placed a ban on the transportation of liquor in any form of for any reason to the frontier. This ban caused a loud outcry, not only from the traders but from the Native Americans. Amherst saw the use of liquor by the natives as counterproductive. He saw the Native Americans as a labor force to be put to work harvesting furs. Anything that kept these people from performing their primary function was to be discouraged. This idea reflected the policies of the Lords of Trade and Plantation in London.[89] But like so many other things in the fur trade, official policy and actual practice were often a world apart, in more ways than one.

While Amherst's ban stopped the flow of alcohol for a time, it did not last. Even while the ban was in effect, contraband goods were still coming into the Great Lakes.

---

[87] Tanner, *Atlas*, p. 6.

[88] Armour & Widder, *Crossroads*, p. 141.

[89] James Adair, *History of the American Indians* (New York: Arno Press, 1930), p. 25.

(Ibid., p. 26.) The most often used procedure was to follow the old French route to Georgian Bay, then avoid the military at Fort Michilimackinac by swinging north to the St. Mary's River. There the contraband was portaged past the small fort by way of the north bank, to be retrieved after the canoes had been inspected.[90]

After 1763, the Lords of Trade and Plantations allowed a certain amount of liquor to be carried by each licensed trader, much as the French had done before them.[91] The English traders found that while a Native American under the influence of alcohol was a danger, a Native American who was deprived of the "English milk"—rum—was an even greater danger.[92]

Although brandy at first had introduced by the French, rum soon became the preferred drink of the native people. Coarse British naval rum was far more potent, and a state of intoxication could be reached more quickly. Rum was demanded as a standard trade good throughout the entire frontier. It was often the first thing a trader would offer as a show of good faith.

Rum was used by the tribes to seal all agreements when dealing with Europeans. (Ibid., p. 163.) While official government policies banned the use of liquor in any form, no council was held, nor treaty signed, without first partaking of large quantities of rum. Often the actual work of the council was held up for several days while waiting for the native participants to sober up enough to talk. (Ibid.) The English often used this to their advantage. Tribal leaders would consummate land deals while in a drunken stupor.[93] The authorities frowned upon such dealings, but they were still legal and binding in an English court of law. During a council a drunken tribal leader could sign away all the hunting lands claimed by his people and have no recourse under the law.

---

[90] Jacobs, *Politics*, p. 55.
[91] O'Callaghan, *DRCHSNY*, Vol. VII, p. 960.
[92] O'Callaghan, *DRCHSNY*, Vol. IX, p. 162.
[93] Jacobs, *Politics*, p. 53.

The elementary question is; why were the Native Americans so taken by the intoxicating effects of alcohol? The answer is really very simple once we examine their religious belief system. Native American religion is based on spiritualism and the belief that the spirit world lies just beyond that of the corporeal. It was believed that the veil between the two could be pierced by attaining a state of altered consciousness. The most often used method of reaching this state was through sleep deprivation or lack of food and water, both of which will result in hallucinations or "visions." The same state was thought to be reached through excessive consumption of alcohol. Liquor, it was believed, could "transport" the user beyond the physical plane to that of the spiritual.[94] Rum and brandy had an immediate effect, compared to several days of deprivation and starvation required by the traditional methods.[95] Through the use of alcohol the native people could "cross over" to the spirit world much more easily and with greater regularity. The addictive effects of liquor also worked to tie the consumer to the trader, his only source of supply. Tribal leaders would request the English to stop the sale of liquor and at the same time ask that their friends might taste it so that "they too may know the joy that it imparts."[96]

The use of liquor became more extensive as contact between the two groups increased. By the end of the eighteenth century the use of alcohol had permeated every age group and every level of native society.[97]

On a formal social level, liquor began to take on a new meaning to the Native American; it began to represent a parental bond between the Europeans and the native people. The Native Americans of the Great Lakes had begun to see the gifts of rum and brandy as "milk," signifying the

---

[94] Jennings, *Iroquois Empire*, p. 318.

[95] Parker, "New Light on Jonathan Carver," *American Magazine and Historical Chronicle* (Vol. 2, No. 1, Spring-Summer, 1986), p. 13.

[96] Adair, *American Indians*, p. 30.

[97] Jacobs, *Politics*, p. 54.

parent/child relationship between the tribes and the Europeans. The native people compared the rum to a mother's milk, given to her children to nurture them. The withholding of such an offering was interpreted by the native "children" as a sign of being abandoned by their European "parents."[98] The native people forced the Europeans to provide alcohol through this ceremonial logic.

Liquor accelerated the breakdown of Native American society and culture. The addictive effects of alcohol were so great that the native people would do anything to gain more of the "English milk." By 1770 it became obvious that any attempt to ban the sale or use of liquor was doomed to failure. No matter what the intention of the British government may have been prior to the takeover of the Great Lakes, it was now evident that liquor was to be a part of the trade.

The governing rules of native society were totally abandoned by those who were under its influence. Liquor had become the perfect consumer good for the fur trade. Not only did it bind the user to the seller but it was cheap to produce and easily transported. Its effects were of a short duration and left the user craving more. Once under its influence the user became the slave of the seller. In his search for the spirit world the Native American had found the final key to the destruction of his own culture.

---

[98] White, "Give us a Little Milk," *Rendezvous*, p. 187.

CHAPTER 9

The American Revolution And The Fur Trade

English attempts to control the turbulent Great Lakes country were met with only limited success for thirteen years. Much of the success they did have was at the expense of their eastern colonies. Such things as the Stamp Act, which was meant to help pay for the war that had gained them this land and the cost of maintaining an army to protect it, as well as the Proclamation of 1763, which would protect it from the expanding eastern population, had raised the ire of the colonists. In response to these and other perceived wrongs, the eastern colonies rose in rebellion. The repercussions of this rebellion would shake the western trade in the Great Lakes to its very foundation.

Prior to the outbreak of the rebellion, the American colonies had been the biggest market for manufactured goods, including beaver hats, cloaks, and other finished products of the western fur trade. With the coming of the rebellion, and the boycott of all English manufactured goods, the English furriers lost a valuable market. This loss of a major market resulted in the glutting of the English and European fur markets, which meant a drop in the value of raw furs.

This meant near economic disaster in the Great Lakes. Many of the traders had financed their operations on credit extended to them by merchants who had received credit from furriers, who now found they had no market for their product. The furs that had been traded for and stored from the previous seasons were now nearly worthless. The price of manufactured trade goods from England had risen, but the native hunter, who neither understood nor cared about European economics, was unwilling to pay a higher price for the goods he needed. The trader, who was caught in the middle, now found himself the victim of a war he did not understand.

Such men as John Askin of Michilimackinac, who had made a fortune in the trade already, could possibly weather this storm, but the small independent traders who lived from season to season were bound to lose all they had.

Many of these men, bitter due to the loss of their livelihood, turned to the military. These veterans of the frontier trade were a valuable asset to the British military in waging their western campaigns. Many were formed into militia companies or were used as interpreters for military negotiations with the Native Americans.

The British had learned an invaluable lesson in the Seven Years' War—it was better to fight with the Native Americans than against them. With native levies to fight for them the British could conduct a two-front war in America. This was a point that was not lost on the new American Congress. Once again the Native Americans found two opposing powers vying for their favor. The western lands of the colonies were important as a food supply to the army of the new republic. The Native Americans would prove invaluable to the British in cutting off this food supply with their skill in hit-and-run warfare. It was an easy task to convince many of the Eastern tribes to fight on behalf of the British, due to the mounting pressure from American colonists for land in the east. It was no small feat to impress on the western tribes the importance of fighting of the side of the English in the west.[99]

The tribes of the Great Lakes knew of the past consequences of fighting on the wrong side in a war. They could see no immediate danger to them in this conflict, until they were reminded that eastern settlers had already moved

---

[99] Askin Papers, p. 375.

in south of the Ohio River. The land of Kentucky had been the common hunting ground of many peoples, including the people of the Great Lakes. This agreed-upon no-mans-land had proven to be the emergency food source for many different tribal groups. Its lack of permanent habitants had made occupation easy for the land-hungry colonists. Yet, even this threat seemed small to the people of the Great Lakes. The British agents were quick to point out that it would not be long before new settlers would move north into the Great Lakes if England were to lose the war. Even this fear did little to sway many of the tribes into taking an active part in the war. Many were willing to provide a nominal number of men to fight, if the young men wished to go, but the vast majority saw no need to fight. It was not until George Rogers Clark attacked the Illinois country that the native people saw the threat as being real.

The threat was very real to the French inhabitants of the Great Lakes. Many of the American revolutionaries in the east were the same people who opposed the Quebec Act which gave the French the right to their own religion and culture. The French feared that if Canada and the Northwest were lost to the Americans, they would lose their rights. French militia companies were formed at Detroit, Vincennes, De Chartres and other forts. Many of these men were displaced *engagés* or *voyageurs* from the fur trade.[100]

Property that belonged to the fur traders was also pressed into service in the war effort. The British took ships such as the *Welcome* and the *Beaver* for their own use on the Great Lakes. The use of these ships benefited the military, but slowed the transportation of the meager supply of trade goods and furs to a crawl.[101]

The Native Americans were not the only ones who were alarmed by Clark's raid. The British feared that Clark would press his advance north to Detroit and even Michilimackinac.

---

[100] James, *License*, p. 114.
[101] Hay, *Michigan Pioneer*, Vol. IX, pp. 366-67.

Nothing could be done to ensure the safety of Detroit, but Michilimackinac was different. It had never been intended to withstand a large-scale military attack. The British decided to abandon the old French fort and relocate to a more defensible position on Mackinaw Island. With the relocation of the military went the relocation of the fur trade. Mackinaw Island and the new fortification would become the hub of the western fur trade well into the next century.

While the Great Lakes themselves were not involved in the actual conflict, they proved to be of great benefit in staging attacks to the east and south. As an incentive to the Native Americans, the rumor was circulated that Governor Hamilton was paying bounties for enemy scalps and prisoners. It can be debated as to whether or not Hamilton was paying for scalps. It is known that he did buy a number of prisoners, however. It is well known that Hamilton supplied many of England's Great Lakes allies for raids into the Ohio country.[102]

All of the traders in the Great Lakes were feeling the pressure of the war. This pressure, added to that from the Hudson's Bay Company, brought about the formation of the Northwest Company. Competition for furs had steadily increased after 1763. The outbreak of the American Revolution and the closing of markets had forced many of the independent traders out of business. Those few traders with enough personal wealth to hold out, such as John Askin, Alexander Henry and others were going to go bankrupt if they could not come to terms among themselves. The result was a loose partnership at first, which was grew into the Northwest Company. For the first time in its history the Hudson's Bay Company was being challenged by a competitor that could begin to equal it in resources and manpower. The British military now found its civilian associates warring against one another for control of the western fur trade.

---

[102] De Peyster, *Michigan Pioneer*, Vol. IX, pp. 329-23.

The independents—those who were able to struggle along—were being forced out of the market entirely by the war and the warring giants of the trade. Smuggling became the only way to survive once again. This time the roles were reversed. The English traders were now forced to smuggle their furs down the Ohio and Mississippi to the French and the Americans. Those who dared to defy the British military and their Native American allies found a lucrative market among the Americans.[103]

Once the French had entered the war as America's allies, an even greater market opened to the independents by way of St. Louis. The English found themselves at a loss to counter this illicit trade. With the demands of the war in the east, they lacked the manpower to stop the flow of furs south. The native hunters cared little where the goods they needed came from, as long as the prices were low. They did little to stop the English independents from trading with the enemy. The result was an ever-growing loss of revenue for the mother country.

This war was a true dilemma. It was a war that brought them nothing good. It was a war that they neither wanted nor understood. The idea of civil war was beyond their comprehension. The native people could understand making war against one's enemies or even against one's former allies, but for a tribe to war amongst itself, which is how they viewed the Revolution, was unthinkable. In their culture, if a group decided to split off from the rest and go their own way, it was their right. There was no good to come from warring amongst one's own people. This was not seen as war, but rather as murder. The only gain that the Native Americans could see in this war was to be paid to fight or stay neutral. If the two sides were willing to give the people gifts, it only made up for what they lost in trade.

---

[103] "Abstracts and Index of Indian Trade Licenses, 1763-1776," Vol. X, p. 44.

The British military, which had followed a policy of limited gift-giving thirteen years earlier, now found themselves in a position of having to flood the Great Lakes with gifts. These gifts were not only in payment for the warriors supplied by the tribes, but also for the support of the tribes themselves. The native people had found by the late 1770's, that they had become totally dependent on the English for the necessities of day-to-day life. With the slowing of the fur trade, the British found that they had to support the people they had sought to dominate. To the native people this meant the end to a long held dream. The day that had been once dreamt of, when they could drive the Europeans form their land forever and return to the old ways was gone forever. Their fate had now been sealed.

The signing of the Treaty of 1783 found the Native Americans of the Great Lakes betrayed by their European allies once again.[104] Even though they had taken only a limited part in the actual fighting of the war, their lands were to be forfeited.

Even those who had fought for the new country found they were not wanted here. The Iroquois, many of whom had fought for the Americans, now found that no distinction was made between themselves, and those of their nation who had fought for the British. The land that the British had claimed was now claimed by the new government of the United States.

Although the official transfer of power was to be immediate, the actual removal of the British would require another uprising and a war. Politically, the Great Lakes had been ceded to the new republic, but economically they still belonged to England. The Treaty of 1783 gave control of the land to America, but England still had use of the all-important waterways. The important military garrisons and trading posts may have been lost, but new posts could be

---

[104] Lord Germain, *Wisconsin Historical Collection*, Vol. II, pp. 175-177.

opened within miles of the new border. New outposts, such as Amherst and St. Joseph Island, began to take the place of those lost in the war. The only thing missing was a central point for control of the western trade, to replace the loss of Mackinaw Island. It was not long before a new post was founded. The rights to this new crossroads fell to the Northwest Company, with the establishment of Fort William, near the Grand Portage at the western end of Lake Superior. From here the Company could control much of the western fur trade and access the Great Plains from the north, while circumventing the Ohio-Mississippi trade routes.

The Northwest Company was not about to give up the trade that they fought so hard to gain. Even if they had lost their key posts in the lake country, they could still move south and pillage the Great Lakes country at will. Employees of the company were encouraged to apply for, and were given , licenses by the American government to trade for furs in the Great Lakes.[105] With the backing of the Northwest Company, and their former ties to the region, they were able to strip the land clean of most of the remaining furs. This practice became so lucrative that a new branch of the Northwest Company was formed, called the Southeasterners.[106] Even after the Northwest was officially given up in 1796, much of the revenue from the Great Lakes went to the British. Once again, with the American takeover of the Great Lakes, the fur trade was to become a government operation. The United States established government licensed and operated "factories." These fur factories were established to maintain control over the trade in illegal liquor and to establish a set price for the furs, not to mention bring in added revenue to the government itself. The factory system proved to be a dismal failure, however. The pressure for the Southeasterners, as well as their main competition in the

---

[105] James, *License*, p. 132.
[106] Bruce Hutchison, *Struggle for the Border* (New York: Longmans, Green and Co., 1955), p. 60.

trade, John Astor's American Fur Company, proved to be too much for the ill-stocked and over-priced government factories.[107] The pillaging of the Great Lakes furs drove most of the Native Americans west and north in search of new hunting grounds. Those who remained became wards of the United States government and were forced to cede their lands bit by bit to the government by treaty. Their society and culture faded to a mere shadow of what they had been previous to European contact.

---

[107] Ibid.

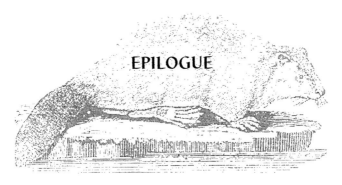

EPILOGUE

The European occupation and exploitation of the Great Lakes lasted for over two hundred years, and the effects on native cultures would be felt for the next two hundred. Their rule, both French and British, was marked by mismanagement, misunderstanding, and corruption. Both great colonial powers had controlled thousands of square miles of territory, a territory occupied by a people that they neither understood, nor cared about. Neither government had any conception of the vast amount of land to which they laid claim, nor did they understand the vast problems in controlling such vast tracts of land. It was this inability to understand the basic problems of the land and its people that led to the mismanagement of the territory during the fur trade era.

The people who occupied this land were so alien to the Europeans, that any understanding between these two groups was impossible. The gaps, both cultural and spiritual, were just too great for either side to bridge. With no basis for understanding, or common cultural ground, the outcome of the fur trade was inevitable. The Europeans and all that they brought with them were the agents of change. The transformation that the fur trade was to bring about would leave no one unchanged. For the Native Americans this metamorphosis was most dramatic. The active subversion of their culture was an intricate part of the fur trade, if not a necessity. In order to harvest the furs that were so important to the trade, a market must be created for goods that the Native American could not manufacture for himself. These goods were not forced on the Native American—they were accepted and even eagerly sought after. This receptive behavior on the part of the native people made them full partners in the destruction of their own culture. The outgrowth of this acceptance was dependence, and with it came the demise of cultural identity, independence, and, in the end, removal from tribal lands.

With that first exchange of goods on that nameless shore so long ago came the opening of Pandora's Box for the Native American, and like that box of ancient legend, once opened it could not be closed. The native people found that along with dependence on the fur trade and the economic advantages it had to offer, there came political dependence in the form of alliances with the Europeans. These alliances forever tied their fates with those of their European allies. These alliances placed the native people in the position of conquest by proxy. They had literally sold themselves into serfdom to the Europeans who viewed them as nothing more than a usable labor force. The Native Americans found, by the end of the colonial period, that they had gone from masters of the land and its resources, who could demand tribute for its use, to tenants who labored for a foreign master.

The poor French farmers and soldiers, who had colonized this strange new land, were also touched by the fur trade and the change it wrought. To these strangers on a foreign shore, the fur trade offered freedom and a release from the crushing feudal system of Old World. Along with the freedom came untold riches for those who were bold enough to harvest them. A common Frenchman could amass more wealth in a single season then he could ever dream of making in a lifetime as a farmer or a common workman. The vast wilderness offered a sense of freedom unmatched by anything that could be found anywhere else under French rule. It has been said that the French Canadian loved the Native American. It was not the Native American people that the Canadian loved but the freedom and potential riches that their way of life offered.

To the government of France, the fur trade meant a way of supporting its colony, while continuing the search for the ·ecer-elusive Northwest Passage. The discovery of this mythical sea route to the orient, it was believed, would assure France world trade dominance. Instead of producing wealth, the colony became a drain on the resources and manpower of New France, as well as the mother country. The constant warfare, with its growing demands for gifts to native allies and the payment for the right to trade, would be a contributing factor to the downfall of the French monarchy.

The fall of New France to the English brought about new problems for its people. Like the Native Americans, the French Canadians found themselves subjects to a new master. Those who were once the masters of the trade, now found themselves servants. The French, unlike the Native Americans, were promised cultural and religious freedom. This freedom came at a high price. The French Canadians would find themselves relegated to the role of second class citizens from that day forward.

The English, like the native people and the French before them, would find their world forever changed by the fur trade. The acquisition of the vast expanse of land, ceded by France was to prove an even greater problem to the English, the final recipients of the fur trade during the colonial period. With the supposed subjugation of the French Canadians and the Native Americans came the difficulties of control and regulation, both of which proved to be impossible. In an effort to generate the maximum amount of revenue from the native work force, the new lands were designated as off-limits to settlement. This and the promise of religious freedom for the French Canadians, would be contributing causes to the loss of the newly gained territory. The English, like the French before them, found the fur trade to be a constant drain, rather than a source of revenue. The Native Americans, who were once given gifts as tribute, were now given gifts to support them as laboring serfs. The English found, like the French, that the vastness of the territory and the easy access to it, made control impossible. Total control of the fur trade meant an increase in problems and a loss in revenue rather than a decrease in problems and an increase in revenue. The English were not fully responsible for the dismantling of Native American cultures, but were the final actors in a long-running tragedy.

The American Revolution spelled the end of the colonial period in the Great Lakes, but not the policies that it had fostered. The new republic adopted wholesale many of the policies developed by the English, particularly those concerning the Native Americans. The British policy of separation and containment, as seen in the Proclamation of 1763, still exists in the modern reservation system. The process of cultural suicide had progressed to removal of tribal identity. The modern welfare system has replaced the gift-giving. Alcohol abuse is still one of the major problems faced by the Native Americans. The seeds that were planted two hundred years ago have borne fruit today. The Native Americans of the Great Lakes are a people who gave up their history and culture for the advantages of an alien world, which had no use for them after the demise of the fur trade.

The colonial fur trade, which had promised wealth and freedom, proved to be a mixed blessing to all involved. The changes that it brought are far reaching, especially in regard to Native American life and culture, and may never be fully understood in their importance.

BIBLIOGRAPHY

Primary Sources

"Abstracts and Index of Indian Trade Licenses, 1763-1776, Sample of Licenses," Public Archives of Canada, Microfilm copy in Minnesota Historical Society.

Amherst, Jeffrey. Papers. W.L. Clements Library, Ann Arbor.

Askin, John. Papers. Saginaw Genealogical Society Library.

Askin, John. Blotters and Ledgers. Burton Collection, Detroit Public Library.

Burnett, William. Day Book and Blotter. Northern Indiana Historical Society, South Bend.

Colden, Cadwallader. Letters and papers, 1760-1776. W.L. Clements Library, Ann Arbor.

"Consolidated Returns of Indian Trade Licenses, 1777-1790," Canada MSS G, Public Archives of Canada.

Craft Papers. W.L. Clements Library, Ann Arbor.

Dodge, John. Papers. Burton Collection, Detroit Public Library.

Gage, General Thomas. Papers. W.L. Clements Library, Ann Arbor.

Haldimand, Lt. Governor. Papers. W.L. Clements Library, Ann Arbor.

Hay, Jehu. Diary, 1763-1765. W.L. Clements Library, Ann Arbor.

History of the Quarters of the Globe, Vol. VII. 1792-1793. W.L. Clements Library, Ann Arbor.

Howell Letters 1777-1798. W.L. Clements Library, Ann Arbor.

Michigan Collection, 1761-1947. W.L. Clements Library, Ann Arbor.

Miscellaneous Manuscripts. (14). Sir Francis Bernard, Esq., W.L. Clements Library, Ann Arbor.

Northwest Territory Collection 1786-1816. W.L. Clements Library, Ann Arbor.

Rogers-Roche Collection. W.L. Clements Library, Ann Arbor.

Shelburne Papers, 1665-1797. W.L. Clements Library, Ann Arbor.

Sterling, James. Letter Book, 1761-1777, Fur Trader from Detroit. W.L. Clements Library, Ann Arbor.

Townshend, Charles. The Letter of, 1725-1767. W.L. Clements Library, Ann Arbor.

Wilson Papers. W.L. Clements Library, Ann Arbor.

Wisconsin Historical Collections. University of Wisconsin, Madison.

Journals and Papers in Print

Bougainville, Louis Antoine de. *Adventure in the Wilderness: The American Journals of Louis Antoine de Bougainville, 1756-1760.* Edited by Edward P. Hamilton. Norman: University of Oklahoma Press, 1964.

Bouquet, Henry. *An Historical Account of the Expedition Against the Ohio Indians in the Year 1764 Under the Command of Henry Bouquet, Esq.: Colonel of Foot and now Brigadier General in America.* London: William Bradford, 1765.

Bouquet, Henry. *The Papers and Journals of Henry Bouquet.* London: William Bradford. 1765.

Carver, Jonathan. *The Journals of Jonathan Carver and Related Documents. 1766-1770.* Edited by John Parker. St. Paul, Minn.: Minnesota Historical Society Press, 1976.

Henry, Alexander. *A Journal of Voyages and Travels in the Interior of North America*. Ann Arbor, MI: University Microfilm, Inc., 1966.

Joutel, Henri. *A Journal of La Salle's Last Voyage*. New York: Corinth Books, 1962.

Labaree, Leonard W. *Royal Instructions to British Colonial Governors 1670-1776*, Vol. II. New York: Octagon Books, Inc., 1967.

LaFrance, Joseph. 'Narrative,' in Report, Houses of Parliament, Report from the Committee Appointed to Enquire into the State and Condition of the Countries.

Laws of the North West Territory. 1792-1796. Law Library, University of Michigan, Ann Arbor.

McDonald, John. *The Diary of John McDonald*. St. Paul: Minnesota Historical Society, 1965.

McLeod, Archibald. *The Diary of Archibald McLeod*. St. Paul: Minnesota Historical Society, 1965.

MacKinzie, Alexander. *Voyages from Montreal on the River St. Laurence*. Ann Arbor: University Microfilms Inc., 1966.

Michigan Pioneer and Historical Society Collections. Lansing, MI: Michigan Historical Society, 1892, 1897.

O'Callaghan, E.B., ed. *Documents Relating to the Colonial History of the State of New York*. Vols. 6-10. Albany, New York: Weed, Parson, and Co., 1957.

Pond, Peter. *The Journals of Peter Pond*. St. Paul: Minnesota Historical Society, 1965.

Secondary Sources

Adair, James. *History of the American Indians*. New York: Arno Press, 1930.

Armour, David A. and Widder, Keith R. *At the Crossroads: Michilimackinac During the American Revolution.* Mackinac Island State Park Commission, Mackinac Island, 1986.

Beckles, Willson. *The Great Company.* London, 1899.

Berkhofer, Robert F. Jr. *The White Man's Indian: Images of The American Indian from Columbus to the Present.* New York: Alfred A. Knopf, 1987.

Biggar, H.P. *The Early Trade Companies of New France: A Contribution to the History of Commerce and Discovery in North America.* Universtiy of Toronto Studies in History. Toronto, 1901.

Billington, Ray Allen. *Land of Savagery, Land of Promise: The European Image of the American Frontier in the Nineteenth Century.* New York: W.W. Norton and Co., 1981.

Brown, Jennifer S.H. *Strangers in Blood: Fur Trade Company Families in Indian Country.* Vancouver: University of British Columbia Press, 1940.

Chittenham, Hiram M. *The American Fur Trade of the Far West.* New York, 1902.

Copway, George (Kah-ge-ga-gah-bowh). *The Traditional History and Characteristic Sketches of the Ojibway Nation.* London: C. Gilpin, 1850, Reprinted Boston: Benjamin B. Mussey and Co., 1851.

Coues, E., ed. *New Light on the Early History of the Greater Northwest: The Manuscript Journal of Alexander Henry, Fur Trader of the Northwest Company, and of David Thompson, Official Geographer and Explorer of the Same Company.* Reprinted edition. Minneapolis: Ross and Haines, 1965.

Dobbs, Arthur. *An Account of the Countries Adjoining to Hudson's Bay in the Northwest Part of America.* London, 1744.

Driver, Harold. *Indians of North America.* Chicago: University of Chicago Press, 1961.

Eccles, W.J. *The Canadian Frontier, 1534-1760*. Albuquerque: University of New Mexico Press, 1964.

Edmunds, R. David. *The Potawatomis: Keepers of the Fire*. Norman: University of Oklahoma Press, 1978.

Fiske, John. *Historical Writings, New France and New England*. New York: Houghton, Mifflin and Co., 1902.

Francis, Peter D., F.J. Kense; and P.G. Duke, (eds.). *Network of the Past: Regional Interactions in Archeology*. Alberta: The Archeological Association of the University of Calgary, 1981.

Frederickson, N. Jay. *The Covenant Chain, Indian Ceremonial and Trade Silver*. Ottawa Canada: National Museum of Canada, 1980.

Gates, Charles M. *Five Fur Traders of the Northwest*. St. Paul: Minnesota Historical Society, 1965.

Glover, Richard, ed. *David Thompson's Narrative 1784-1812*. Toronto: Champlain Society, 1962.

Hamilton, Milton. *Sir William Johnson: Colonial America, 1715-1763*. Port Washington, N.Y.: Kennikat Press, 1976.

Hutchison, Bruce. *Struggle for the Border*. New York: Longmans, Green and Co., 1955.

Innis, Harold. *The Fur Trade in Canada: An Introduction to Canadian Economic History*. (1930). Rev. ed. prepared by S.D. Clark and W.T. Eastbrook. Toronto: University of Toronto Press, 1956.

Jacobs, Wilber, ed. *The Appalachian Indian Frontier: Edmond Atkin's Report and Plan of 1755*. Lincoln: University of Nebraska Press, 1967.

Jacobs, Wilber R. *Indian Diplomacy and Indian Gifts: Anglo-French Rivalry Along the Ohio and Northwest Frontier*. Stanford, 1950.

Jacobs, Wilber R. *Wilderness Politics and Indian Gifts: The Northern Colonial Frontier 1748-1763*. Lincoln, Nebraska: University of Nebraska Press, 1950.

Jaenen, Cornelius J. *Friend or Foe: Aspects of French-Amerindian Cultural Contact in the Sixteenth and Seventeenth Centuries*. New York: Columbia University Press, 1976.

James, Dorothy V. *License for Empire: Colonialism by Treaty in Early America*. Chicago: University of Chicago Press, 1982.

Jenness, Diamond. *The Indians of Canada*. Ottawa, 1939.

Jennings, Francis. *The Ambiguous Iroquois Empire*. New York: W.W. Norton and Co., 1984.

_____. *Empire of Fortune: Crowns, Colonies and Tribes in the Seven Year's War in America*. New York: W.W. Norton and Co., 1988.

Jones, Dorothy V. *License for Empire: Colonialism by Treaty in Early America*. Chicago: University of Chicago Press, 1982.

Kennedy, J.H. *Jesuit and Savage in New France*. New Haven: Yale University Press, 1950.

Kinietz, W. Vernon. *Indians of the Western Great Lakes*. Ann Arbor: University of Michigan Press, 1965.

Kohl, Johann G. *Kitchi-Gami: Life Among the Lake Superior Ojibway*. St. Paul, Minn.: Minnesota Historical Society Press, 1985.

Kupperman, Karen Ordahl. *Settling with the Indians: The Meeting of English and Indian Cultures in America, 1580-1640*. Totowa, N.J.: Rowan and Littlefield, 1980.

Leach, Douglas E. *The Northern Colonial Frontier 1607-1763*. New York: Holt, Rinehart, and Winston, 1966.

McCusker, John J. *Money and Exchange in Europe and America 1600-1775*. Chapel Hill, N.C., 1978.

Martin, Calvin. *Keepers of the Game: Indian-Animal Relationships and the Fur Trade*. Berkeley: University of California Press, 1978.

Newman, Peter C. *Company of Adventures*. Vol. I. Viking Penguin Inc. New York, N.Y., 1985.

Nute, Grace Lee. *The Voyageur*. St. Paul: Reprinted Edition, Minnesota Historical Society, 1955.

Orchard, William. *Beads and Beadwork of the American Indian*. New York: Museum of the American Heye Foundation, 1975.

Parkman, Francis. *The Conspiracy of Pontiac and the Indian War after the Conquest of Canada*. (1851). Rev. New Library ed. Boston: Little, Brown and Co., 1909.

_____, *Count Frontenac and New France under Louis XIV*. (1877) New Library ed. Boston: Little, Brown and Co., 1909.

_____, *A Half Century of Conflict* (1892) Boston: Little, Brown and Co., 1909.

_____, *The Jesuits in North America in the Seventeenth Century*. (1867). New Library ed. Boston: Little, Brown and Co., 1909.

_____, *Montcalm and Wolfe*. (1884) 2 vols. New Library ed. Boston: Little, Brown and Co., 1909.

Pease, T.C. *Anglo-French Boundary Disputes in the West 1749-1763*. Springfield, Ill., 1936.

Peckham, Howard. *Pontiac and the Indian Uprising*. New York: Russell and Russell Publishing, 1964.

Peckham, Howard, and Charles Gibson, eds. *Attitudes of Colonial Powers Toward the Native Americans*. Salt Lake City: University of Utah Press, 1969.

Quimby, George I. *Indian Culture and European Trade Goods*. Madison: University of Wisconsin Press, 1966.

Ray, Arthur J. *Indians in the Fur Trade: Their Role as Hunters, Trappers and Middlemen in the Lands Southwest of Hudson Bay.* Toronto: University of Toronto Press, 1974.

Rich, E.E. *The History of the Hudson's Bay Company, 1670-1870.* 2 vols. London: Hudson's Bay Record Society Publications, 21, 22; 1958-1959.

Russell, Carl P. *Guns on the Early Frontier.* Berkeley: University of California Press, 1947.

Russell, Howard S. *Indian New England Before the Mayflower.* Hanover, N.H.: University Press of New England, 1980.

Russell, Nelson. *The British Regime in Michigan and the Old North-West 1760-1796.* Chicago: Porcupine Press, 1979.

Sosin, Jack M. *Whitehall and the Wilderness: The Middle West in British Colonial Policy.* New York: Greenwood Press, 1961.

Tanner, Helen H. *Atlas of Great Lakes Indian History.* Norman: University of Oklahoma Press, 1986.

Thistle, Paul C. *Indian-European Trade Relations in the Lower Saskatchewan River Region to 1840.* Manitoba: The University of Manitoba Press, 1986.

_____, ed. *The Jesuit Relations and Allied Documents.* Reprinted ed. New York: Greenwood Press, 1959.

Thwaites, Reuben G. ed. *Early Western Travels 1748-1846 a Series of Some of the Best and Rarest Contemporary Volumes of Travels Descriptions of the Aborigines and Economic Conditions in the Middle and Far West during the Period of Early American Settlement.* Vols. I, II. New York: AMS Press Inc., 1966.

Trelease, Allen W. *Indian Affairs in Colonial New York.* Ithaca, 1960.

Turner, Frederick J. *The Character and Influence of the Indian Trade in Wisconsin: A Study of the Trading Post as an Institution.* Norman: University of Oklahoma Press, 1977.

Tyrrell, J.B. ed. *Journals of Samuel Hearne and Philip Turnor between 1774-1792.* Toronto: Champlain Society, 1934.

Vandivar, Clarence A. *The Fur-Trade and the Early Western Exploration.* New York: Copper Square Publishing, 1971.

Wallace, W.S., ed. *Documents Relating to the Northwest Co.* Toronto: University of Toronto Press, 1934.

Waller, G.M. *Samuel Vetch: Colonial Enterpriser.* Published For the Institute of Early American Culture. Chapel Hill: University of North Carolina Press, 1960.

Williams, Gyndwr, ed. *Andrew Graham's Observations on Hudson's Bay, 1767-1791.* London: Hudson's Bay Records Society, 1969.

Articles

Briggs, Winstonley "Le Pays de Illinois." *William and Mary Quarterly,* January 1990, Vol. XLVII, no. 1.

Canny, Nicholas P. "The Ideology of English Colonization From Ireland to America," *William and Mary Quarterly,* 3rd. ser. XXX 1973.

Cutcliffe, Stephen H. "Colonial Indian Policy as a Measure of Rising Imperialism: New York and Pennsylvania, 1700-1750." *Western Pennsylvania Historical Magazine,* 64:3 (July 1981), pp. 237-68.

Eccles, W.J. "La Mer de l'Ouest: Outpost of Empire," *Rendezvous, Selected Papers of the Fourth North American Trade Conference, 1981.* St. Paul: Minnesota Historical Society Press, 1984.

Eid, Leroy V. "The Ojibwa-Iroquois War: The War the Five Nations Did Not Win." *Ethnohistory,* 26:4 (Fall 1979), pp. 297-342.

Ellis, George E. "The Red Indian of North America in Contact with the French and the English." In *Narrative and Critical History of America,* ed. Justin Wisor. 8 vols. Boston: Houghton, Mifflin and Co., 1889. 1:283-328.

Jenks, Albert E. "The Wild Rice Gatherers of the Upper Lakes." *Annual Report of the Bureau of American Ethnology*, pt. 2 (1901), 1013-1137.

Jennings, Francis. "Jacob Young: Indian Trader and Interpreter." In *Struggle and Survival in Colonial America*. Edited by David G. Sweet and Gary Nash. Berkeley: University of California Press, 1981.

Judd, Carol M. and Arthur J. Ray, eds. *Old Trails and New Directions: Papers of the Third North American Fur Trade Conference*. Toronto: Toronto University Press, 1980.

Lowie, Robert. "The Assiniboine." *Anthropological Papers of the Museum of Natural History*, 4 (1909), 1-270.

Lunn, Jean. "The Illegal Fur Trade out of New France 1713-1760." *Canadian Historical Association Report* (1939).

Martin, Calvin. "The Metaphysics of Writing Indian-White History." *Ethnohistory*, 26/2 (Spring 1979).

Nash, Gary B. "The Free Society of Traders and the Early Politics of Pennsylvania." *Pennsylvania Magazine of History and Biography*, 89:2 (April 1965), pp. 3-7.

Parker, John. "New Light on Jonathan Carver," *The American Magazine and Historical Chronicle*. Vol. 2, No. 1, Spring-Summer, 1986.

Pritchett, J.P. "Some Red River Fur Trade Activities." *Minnesota Historical Bulletin*, 5 (1924), pp. 401-23.

Reid, Allana G. "Intercolonial Trade During the French Regime." *Canadian Historical Review*, Vol. XXXII, (Sept. 1951).

Rich, E.E. "Trade Habits and Economic Motivation among the Indians of North America." *Canadian Journal of Economics and Political Science*, 27 (1960) pp. 35-53.

Rogers, E.S. "The Hunting Group-Hunting Territory Complex Among the Mistassini Indians." *National Museum of Canada, Bulletin.* No. 195, Ottawa, 1963.

____, "Southern Ojibwa." In *Northeast,* pp. 760-71.

Ruggles, Richard I. "The Historical Geography and Cartography of the Canadian West, 1678-1795." Ph.D. Dissertation, University of London, 1958.

Smith, Donald B. "Who Are the Mississauga?" *Ontario History,* 17:4 (Dec. 1975). pp. 211-22.

Swagerty, William R. "Marriage and Settlement Patterns of Rocky Mountain Trappers and Traders." *Western Historical Quarterly,* 11:2 (April 1980), pp. 159-80.

Trelase, Allen W. The Iroquois and the Western Fur Trade: A Problem in Interpretation." *Mississippi Valley Historical Review,* 49 (1962), pp. 32-51.

Trigger, Bruce G. "The Destruction of Huronia: A Study in Economic and Cultural Change, 1609-1650." *Transactions of the Royal Canadian Institute,* 33 (1960), pp. 14-45.

White, Bruce M. "'Give us a Little Milk': The Social and Cultural Significance of Gift Giving in the Lake Superior Fur Trade." *Rendezvous, Selected Papers of the Fourth North American Fur Trade Conference, 1981.* St. Paul: Minnesota Historical Society Press, 1984.

Worcester, Donald E. and Thomas F. Schilz. "The Spread of Firearms Among the Indians on the Anglo-French Frontier." *American Indian Quarterly,* Vol. VIII #2 (Spring 1984).

INDEX